·SoFT·
FURNISHINGS

OVER 65 STEP-BY-STEP PROJECTS
FOR YOUR HOME

·SOFT· FURNISHINGS

OVER 65 STEP-BY-STEP PROJECTS FOR YOUR HOME

Contributors

Anna Carrick Smith • Rosamund Forester

Jenny Gibbs • Caroline Hope

Charyn Jones • Jacqueline Venning

BROCKHAMPTON PRESS
LONDON

CONTENTS

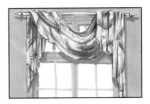

Note: Where English terminology differs from the
American, the English descriptions are given in brackets.

First published in the UK
1992 by Cassell
Wellington House
125 Strand
London
WC2R 0BB

This edition published 1998 by Brockhampton Press,
    a member of Hodder Headline PLC Group

ISBN 1 86019 8821

Produced by Rosemary Wilkinson
in association with Weldon Russell Pty Ltd
43 Victoria Street, McMahons Point,
Sydney NSW 2060, Australia

Design: Patrick Knowles
Editing: Charyn Jones
Special photography: Mark Gatehouse
Illustrations: Richard Draper
Picture research: Shona Wood

British Library Cataloguing-in-Publication Data
A catalogue record for this book is available from the
British Library

Typeset by Fakenham Photosetting Limited

Printed at Oriental Press, Dubai, U.A.E.

INTRODUCTION

Decorating an interior with soft furnishings, whether an elaborate window treatment or a color-coordinated set of cushions and covers, is one of the most attractive, versatile, and universally popular ways of creating a personal style in the home. These fabric-based furnishings can be expensive to commission, however they are also immensely satisfying to design and make yourself – a wonderful way to channel your creative energies. This book brings together a number of experts, who contribute chapters on their own specialist areas. Three of these guest authors, including myself, are from KLC, a leading school of interior design and decoration in the U.K.

Jacqueline Venning, who wrote the chapters on curtains and shades (blinds), runs introductory curtain making courses at KLC and teaches soft furnishing and upholstery at college level. Caroline Hope is a highly experienced international interior decorator, who specializes in soft furnishings. She has written about cushions and beds and has also compiled "The Workroom", a chapter describing the basic equipment needed and an A to Z of fabric types. The chapter on chair covers comes from Rosamund Forester, who runs a very successful soft furnishings business, collaborating with interior designers, and Anna Carrick Smith brings her specialist knowledge of lampshades. She undertakes a wide variety of commissions to make lampshades, including special projects for historic houses. Charyn Jones, who describes a range of different table treatments, is already an established author on the subject of soft furnishings.

This is not only a practical book with clear, easy-to-follow instructions and step-by-step photographs, but also a source of inspiration. In my own three chapters I have presented a variety of design ideas for different windows, rooms and styles, which I hope will give readers interest, pleasure and enthusiasm for projects of their own.

Jenny Gibbs
Principal, KLC
Interior Design Training

CUSHIONS

CUSHIONS

*C*ushions have been used for centuries for comfort, even in the early days when the bed was only a slab of marble. We have moved on from that; a wide variety of cushions has evolved, and these styles combined can produce a riot of color and enhance the feeling of comfort and relaxation in a room. They can be used in many ways. Armchairs and sofas often benefit from a variety of soft cushions that fit neatly into the small of the back, while a large floor cushion can serve as another chair. Similarly, a hard bolster can double as the armrests or headboard on a bed.

Cushions are economical soft furnishing projects because they are generally made from the remnants and endcuts of the curtain fabric. However, they are most useful in bringing the room together by combining many colors and textures. A simple contrast will often give the curtain fabric more impact. If you see a piece of attractive fabric, or even a tapestry or embroidery, it may be perfect to add to those already there, thereby building up a nice collection of shapes, styles, and sizes. Because of the small amounts involved, you may even be tempted by a more expensive fabric.

Cushions are wonderful as the first items in a completely bare room, without any scheme at all, providing instant color. They are also the simplest method of co-ordinating an existing scheme. Whatever shape, color, or fabric used, depending on how they are made and arranged, they will add comfort, style, and elegance where needed.

FABRIC

The choice of fabrics is enormous but some attention should be paid to their use. Shimmering silks, embroidery, tapestry, and antique velvets, contemporary abstracts, handpainted and patchwork designs, as well as weaves in bold designs and colors and almost all cotton chintzes look good in a mass. Dressmaker fabrics can be made up into delicate cushions but remember they might not wear so well, or silk could fade on the piping, also they might not be substantial enough to take a trim, such as fan edging or fringe. Lightweight fabrics, such as lace, silk, organza, and voile, have to be lined to give more strength. Heavier fabrics such as corduroys, heavy-duty velvets, and linen blends (unions) are used for bolsters and floor cushions, as well as any padded cushions and "bean bags" which will have frequent use.

Handpainted silk should be backed with another fabric to strengthen it. Obviously it should not be subjected to heavy wear; everything has its limitations. Needlepoint and cross-stitch enthusiasts should stretch their work by dampening and tacking it onto a board until dry before using. Ready-made needlepoint and crewelwork are also available.

Needlework panels usually come ready stretched for sewing and can be used in lots of ways – over the whole cushion or as an insert. To display the work best, choose a complementary background. A curtain velvet in one of the colors is an appropriate choice.

Decorative Additions
The more adventurous might like appliqué (see page 110). This is the art of cutting out shapes and sewing them onto another fabric with a decorative stitch on the machine. The raised effect of the motif is pretty and adds interest.

Ruching along the welt is another option. This

is done by gathering the fabric covering the welt and attaching as before. Chair seats look good buttoned; this also strengthens the fabric and it adds to the general appearance and color scheme in the room, especially when coordinating with the piping. The number of buttons added is according to taste.

Cushions vary in size and appearance enormously depending on their trims. A well puffed-up, richly patterned square cushion, caught in at the corners to give a gathered appearance, then piped at the edge or caught in the middle with a rope, is exotically called a Turkish cushion. Cording can also be handsewn along the edge of a square or oblong shape, either tied in knots, or looped at the corners. Similarly, silky tassels sewn into the four corners are effective. Braid can be used extensively as a square in the center or down two sides of an oblong or square cushion.

A fringe, bobbles, or a fan-edged trim sewn into the seam makes an ordinary shape more decorative. They can be laid on and stitched to the top section of the cover before completing the seams, so that they appear like a frame when turned around. When there are no trims, try a self border. Simply make the cover about 2 in (5 cm) larger all round and carefully stitch along the original stitching line. This border can be lightly padded and even topstitched once or twice.

Frills and ruffles can be bound with a small band of color matching the piping, or make two layers of ruffles, laid on the fabric (as shown on page 114) or set into the seams. The choice is yours.

FILLINGS

Most stores hold a good selection of shapes and sizes of ready-made cushion forms (pads) of various fillings and will advise you on their uses. If, however, you wish to make your own cases this can be done in muslin (calico), ticking, cambric, or any other cotton weave, remembering that if using down, a downproof fabric must be used,

preferably with a French seam, and the stitches should be small and sewn with a fine needle. Sew as for the cushion cover, leaving an opening of approximately 6 in (15 cm) for the stuffing. Take care to do this in a draft-free room as it can be an untidy and messy job. In order to make your cushions deliciously plump, make sure your form (pad) is 1 in (2.5 cm) larger than the cover, excluding all frills or finished edges.

The filling will largely depend on the effect required, and as such breaks down into easy categories.

Feather
White and gray are the most readily available and reasonably priced. This stuffing plumps up well and makes lovely cushions.

Down
A much more expensive and luxurious filling, down is used when making very light cushions. It puffs itself up, but make sure that it is encased in a good cambric cover, so that the down does not work its way through. It is often combined with feathers to make a less expensive filling.

Foam
Available in different widths and qualities, foam is suitable for chair cushions (squabs), boxed cushions, and window seats. Make sure that this too has an outer cover as it might crumble in time.

Foam chips
A non-absorbent stuffing, chips can look lumpy if the cover is not filled full enough. They are suitable for use in garden accessories or children's rooms as they are hard wearing and economical.

Polystyrene beads
Used for large floor cushions and "bean bags".

Polyester batting (acrylic and polyester wadding)
This is fully washable and more expensive than foam. Useful for less formal shaped cushions and needs plumping up often.

SQUARE AND RECTANGULAR CUSHIONS

These covers add simple impact when different sizes and colors are used together on the same chair or sofa. They are usually piped, adding a neat edge. This can be in a constrasting color, say a red cushion with green piping beside a green cushion with red piping. Patterned fabrics can also be piped with a plain color picked out of the design and look especially good on a plain sofa. For a softer, more romantic feel, a ruffle (frill) or even two will change the mood of the cushion and surroundings.

The best fastening is a zipper inserted in one of two ways – either straight across the center back, or sewn into the side seam. Silk or lightweight cushions can be slipstitched closed by hand, rather than having a bulky zipper.

— A PIPED CUSHION COVER —

Materials

cushion fabric
cushion form (pad)
tailor's chalk
ruler
matching thread
zipper, snaps, hook and eye
fastening or Velcro*
cord covered in bias strips (see
page 122) in your chosen color

* 4 in (10 cm) shorter than the
width of the finished cushion.

1 Calculate the amount of fabric by measuring the length and width of the form (pad). The cover should be 1 in (2.5 cm) smaller than the form (pad) for a good fit. Measure the four sides and calculate the amount of piping needed.

2 Lay the cushion fabric on a flat surface, and with tailor's chalk and a ruler mark two squares on the straight of the grain to the required measurement. On one of the squares add 1 in (2.5 cm) to one side to allow for the zipper insertion. Make sure any pattern is centered on both pieces.

3 Cut out both pieces, allowing ½ in (12 mm) seam allowance all around the outside edges. Cut the larger piece (for the back) in two.

4 With right sides together, baste (tack) the back panel together leaving a 1 in (2.5 cm) seam allowance. Machine stitch a 2 in (5 cm) seam at both ends of the back panel, leaving the basting (tacking) stitches along the center of the seam. Press seam open.

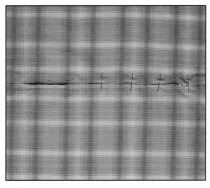

5 Insert the zipper, making certain that it is centered over the seam and along the length of the panel. Turn the fabric to the right side and stitch all round the zipper with the zipper foot on the machine. Remove the basting (tacking) stitches. Open the zipper.

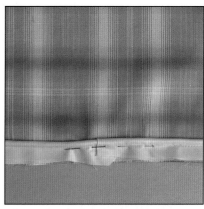

6 Make up the piping (see page 38), and place it all around the front panel on the right side of the fabric with raw edges together.

7 Join the ends of the piping by unpicking a small section and twisting the cord ends together. Overlap the fabric strip to cover the cord, turning back one end so that no raw edges are visible.

8 Pin and stitch the piping to the outside edges of the front panel using the seam allowance line marked on the fabric with tailor's chalk (step 2). Slightly curve the piping at the corners. A zipper foot is useful when stitching this step.

9 Notch and trim the corners to make them more pliable.

10 Place the two cushion pieces together with right sides facing and machine stitch around all four sides with a ½ in (12 mm) seam allowance. Clip all four corners.

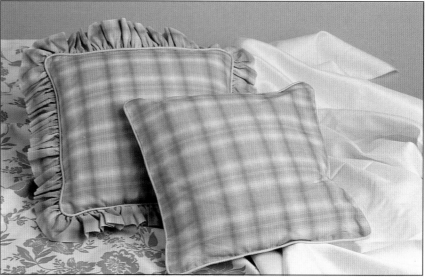

11 Press open the four seams and then turn the cover right side out and press the panels.

12 Insert the cushion form (pad), making sure it goes into the corners. Close the zipper.

Making a Ruffle (Frill)

To make a ruffle or frill for cushions or any other soft furnishing project, you need to decide whether the ruffle (frill) is to be double or single. A double ruffle (frill) is a length of fabric folded in half so the right side of the fabric shows on both sides. A single ruffle (frill) is hemmed and the wrong side of the fabric will be seen. A single ruffle (frill) is ideal for a bulky fabric or when there is no right or wrong side, in which case the hem edge can be bound with commercial or prepared bias binding.

Measure around the cushion perimeter and cut one-and-a-half to three times this length plus seam allowances, depending on the fullness you want. For a double ruffle (frill) the strip should be twice the required depth plus seam allowances.

Sew the two short ends together, press seams open and then fold the fabric lengthwise in half with wrong sides facing.

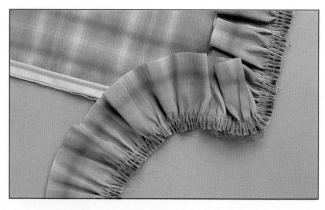

Run two rows of gathering along the raw edges and gather up the fullness, then pin to the cushion panel, distributing the gathers as evenly as possible on each side and gathering slightly more fabric at the corners. Machine along the seam allowance line. When you join the cushion panels, make sure the ruffle (frill) is well toward the center of the cushion, so that it is not caught in the seams. Trim the corners to remove bulk.

ROUND CUSHIONS

These cushions can be ruffled (frilled), braid-trimmed, covered in lace, or simply contrast-piped and will look effective when combined with a selection of square and shaped cushions. The zipper can either go across the center back or in the side of the border. Both methods are described below. Either way it need not be obtrusive. Round cushions can be classy and noticeably chic or delightfully soft and feminine, depending on the choice of fabric.

Materials

cushion fabric	paper for pattern
cushion form (pad)	thin string and pencil
zipper*	
decorative finish, such as a ruffle	* 4 in (10 cm) shorter than the
(frill) or piping	diameter of the finished cushion.
matching thread	

---

1 Calculate the amount of fabric needed by measuring the diameter of the form (pad) and adding ½ in (12 mm) seam allowance all around. You will need more fabric for the piping.

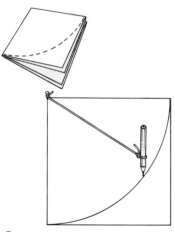

2 Make a paper pattern of the circle by folding a piece of paper into four. Press a pin into the corner of the fold and attach a thread measured to the radius of the cushion plus a seam allowance of ½ in (12 mm). Hold a pencil at the other end of the thread and draw a quarter-circle. A less accurate way is to take a hard ruler and mark out the desired measurement from the corner, slowly turning the ruler and marking as you go. Draw the curved line.

3 Cut around the line on the paper and open out.

4 Place this circular pattern on the fabric, making sure that any pattern is centered. Cut out the top cover.

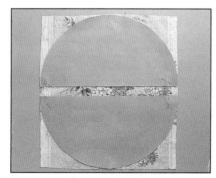

5 Using the same paper pattern, fold in half and cut along the folded line. Place the two pieces on the main fabric and spread 1 in (2.5 cm) apart to allow for the zipper seam. Cut out.

6 Pin the two sections right sides together and raw edges matching, pin, and baste (tack). Continue as for the square cushion cover.

If you want to decorate with a ruffle (frill) and piping, pin and baste (tack) the piping before attaching the ruffle (frill) so that the piping can be seen from the front of the cushion.

To insert a zipper in a piped seam, attach the piping to one panel and with right sides together, stitch for 2 in (5 cm) at either end of the zipper opening.

Open the zipper and place one edge against the piping, with the teeth up against the piping and the upper side of the zipper towards the fabric. Pin and baste (tack). Using the zipper foot, machine stitch along the zipper close to the piping.

Do the same with the other zipper edge. This method allows no stitching to be seen on the right side of the cushion cover, rather like the method used for inserting zippers in lingerie.

SHAPED CUSHIONS

Not all cushions need to be made up in traditional shapes, they can also be shaped as hearts, diamonds, or any shape you wish. Patterns for these are found in most good stores, and the basic sewing is as already described, though the filling should be synthetic.

If you want to make your own design, calculate how much fabric is needed by measuring the pattern drawn, add on the seam allowance, and buy twice the amount. The same amount of lining fabric will be needed for the inner case, which will contain the filling.

Materials

cushion fabric
close weave fabric for lining
polyester batting (wadding) or
foam chips
matching thread
snap fasteners or Velcro
paper for pattern

1 Cut out the paper pattern. If you are planning a heart shape, cut a piece of paper slightly larger than the finished cushion, fold it in half, and draw half a heart against the fold. Cut out and open it up.

2 Allowing ½ in (12 mm) seam allowance all around, cut out two pieces of cushion fabric and two pieces of lining. If you are inserting a zipper across the back, cut the front panel only and then cut the paper pattern in half and place both pieces on the fabric, with a 1 in (2.5 cm) gap for the zipper. Cut out the back panel and cut across where the zipper seam is to go (see page 15).

3 Make up the lining, machine sewing double rows of stitches for strength. Leave an opening to insert the stuffing. Turn right side out.

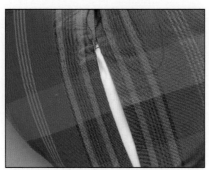

4 Stuff the cushion lining and slipstitch the opening.

5 Continue as for plain cushions.

BOLSTERS

These are normally seen at either end of a sofa or chaise longue and are finished in several ways, the most common being a gathered end with a button or tassel, or a tailored end piped around the circumference.

They were traditionally covered in a white linen case and used on the bed, stretching from one side to the other. They are usually firm, but the type of fabric used will determine whether they are functional or merely decorative. A heavy weave or corduroy is ideal at the end of a sofa or as a headboard, while a rich silk or satin finished in equally sumptuous trims is appropriate in a bedroom, where a crisp contemporary chintz could also be used most effectively.

Sometimes a contrast braid or panels of lace are applied around the circumference of the cover. They are generally finished with a zipper but can be gathered into a draw string at both ends for a more informal setting.

MAKING A TAILORED AND PIPED BOLSTER

Materials

cushion fabric
bolster form (pad)
piping
zipper*
matching thread
decorative tassels, or buttons
covered in the cushion fabric

* 4 in (10 cm) shorter than the length of the bolster form (pad).

1 Measure the length of the cushion form (pad) and its circumference. Cut a rectangular piece of fabric to this size plus ½ in (12 mm) seam allowance all around. Cut a circle of fabric for each end of the bolster, adding the same seam allowance. Check that any pattern is centered on the ends.

2 Fold the rectangle in half with right sides together to make a tube, pin, and stitch seam in from both ends, leaving an opening long enough for the zipper.

3 Press the seam open and pin the zipper in place, making certain that it is centered.

4 Using a double matching thread and a tidy backstitch, stitch the zipper into the seam. Alternatively, machine stitch in place, using the appropriate foot on your machine.

5 Turn the cover to the right side and press. Open the zipper a little. Turn the cover inside out again.

6 Pin the prepared piping onto the two circular ends, matching the raw edges and using the seam allowance as the stitching line. Join the ends of the piping (see step 7, page 13).

7 Carefully fit the circular ends to either end of the cover, pin, and machine stitch with a zipper foot.

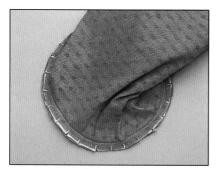

8 Notch both the ends and press in towards the center of the circle.

9 Turn the cover to the right side, press again, and insert the form (pad). A tassel can be applied by hand to the end for added decoration.

MAKING A GATHERED BOLSTER

Materials

cushion fabric
bolster form (pad)
piping
zipper*
matching thread
decorative tassels
two large buttons, covered in the cushion or coordinating fabric

* 4 in (10 cm) shorter than the length of the bolster form (pad).

1 Cut a rectangle of fabric: to the circumference of the form (pad) for the width, and the length of the form plus the radius of the end for the length, allowing ½ in (12 mm) seam allowances.

2 Make up a tube as on page 17 and insert the zipper as before. A zipper is not always necessary; Velcro, snap fasteners, or slipstitching by hand is often all that is required.

3 Turn the cover inside out and press the seam.

4 Turn under a ½ in (12 mm) seam at both ends and machine stitch the hem.

5 With a strong thread, gather up the ends, making sure the stitches are even.

6 Insert the bolster centrally in the tube, then draw in the gathering threads. Finish off with a few good stitches to secure.

7 Sew the buttons over the holes left in the center ends of the bolster. Use a strong thread to secure the button to the bolster form (pad) and also through the fabric, hiding the stitches as you finish. A tassel can be sewn on in the same way but it is only needed on one end of a bolster if it is to form an armrest for a sofa.

ALTERNATIVE GATHERED END

A more sophisticated gathered end can be made for the piped bolster by using a double circle at either end. The reinforcing or inner circle can be made up from another fabric as it will not be seen.

Make as for the bolster cushion on page 17 to step 5. To prepare the gathered ends, cut two rectangles of fabric, the length equal to the circumference of the circle and the width the radius of the circle. Allow for seams.

With right sides facing, machine stitch the two short ends to make a cylinder. Press seam open, and with

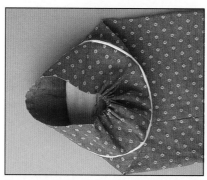

the wrong side of the cylinder against the right side of the inner circle, sew one edge to the reinforcing circle. Snip the seam allowance all around to ease the tension.

Gather up the other edge and pull the gathering thread tight so it lies flat against the inner circle. Cover the exposed gathered end with a button or tassel.

Apply the piping as above and complete the bolster.

CUSHIONS WITH GUSSETS

S quare, rectangular, and round cushions can all be made with a border of fabric called a "gusset" or "welt" running around them to form a box. This gives the cushion a firm, tailored appearance and is more suitable for a medium weight such as cotton, although any fabric can be used. Foam-filled boxed cushions are generally used for window seats, or made into what are known as "squab" or padded seats for occasional chairs.

Foam is the best stuffing when a special shape has to be cut. Premade feather forms (pads) are available. When made up, the cushion cover should be a good fit and finished in the welt with either a zipper, Velcro, or a snap fastening.

MAKING A SQUARE CUSHION WITH GUSSET

Materials

cushion fabric
cushion form (pad)*
matching fabric
zipper†
piping (twice the length of the cushion all around)

* Always cover a foam form (pad) with lining to ensure durability.
† 4 in (10 cm) shorter than the length of the welt

1 Measure the length and width of the cushion and cut two pieces of fabric to these dimensions plus ½ in (12 mm) seam allowance all around.

2 Measure the length and depth of the gussets (welts) and cut three strips of fabric to these measurements plus allowances. Cut the fourth welt strip to the same length but increase the width by 1 in (2.5 cm) for the zipper.

3 Cut the zipper gusset (welt) section in half lengthwise and insert the zipper (see page 13).

4 Machine stitch the four gusset (welt) sections together to fit the cushion form (pad) snugly. Press the seams open and clip the corners.

5 Pin, baste (tack), and machine stitch one length of piping all around one of the cushion panels, using the seam allowance of ½ in (12 mm) as the guideline. Repeat on the other panel.

6 With right sides facing, machine stitch one panel to the gusset (welt) section. The corners should be made sharp by turning the machine needle at right angles. Clip the corners. Open the zipper.

7 Repeat with the other panel.

8 Turn right sides out through the zipper opening and press.

Circular Cushion with Gusset

A circular cushion is made in the same way but with only two sections of gusset (welt); the smaller one holds the zipper or fastening. If the gusset (welt) is cut on the bias it will be easier to fit. Cut plenty of notches around the finished cover so that there is no tension around the circle.

The zipper needs to be long enough to allow the cushion form (pad) or the foam filling through. Make one section of the gusset (welt) 4 in (10 cm) longer than the zipper and the second section to fit the remainder of the circumference plus seam allowances.

The cushions can be piped in a different color as shown in the photograph above.

MAKING A CHAIR CUSHION

For kitchen and hard dining room chairs these thin, foam-filled cushions are the answer. The piping could be made in a contrasting color, or as illustrated here, taking a bias cut of the checked fabric. The cushions are attached to the chair uprights with bows, which are both decorative and practical. They could be made to match the piping. The foam supplier will probably cut the form (pad) to shape, if you take along the paper template.

Materials

cushion fabric
lining fabric
1½ in (4 cm) foam form (pad)*
piping
snap fasteners or Velcro
paper for template

* An alternative form (pad) could be a couple of layers of batting (wadding) between two pieces of lining.

1 Cut a paper template for the seat. Fold the pattern in half, and check that both sides are the same.

2 Place the pattern on the seat to check the fit. It should come right to the edges. Mark the position of the uprights.

3 Using the pattern, cut two pieces of fabric allowing ½ in (12 mm) seam allowance.

4 Cut out a foam form (pad) to fit the chair seat and cover it with lining fabric.

5 Make up the required length of piping (see page 38), pin, baste (tack) and stitch to one piece of the seat cover.

6 Cut two strips of fabric about 24 in (60 cm) long and 2 in (5 cm) wide for the ties. Fold in half lengthwise with right sides together and sew across both ends, and down the side, leaving an opening halfway along. Turn right side out and press. Slipstitch the opening closed.

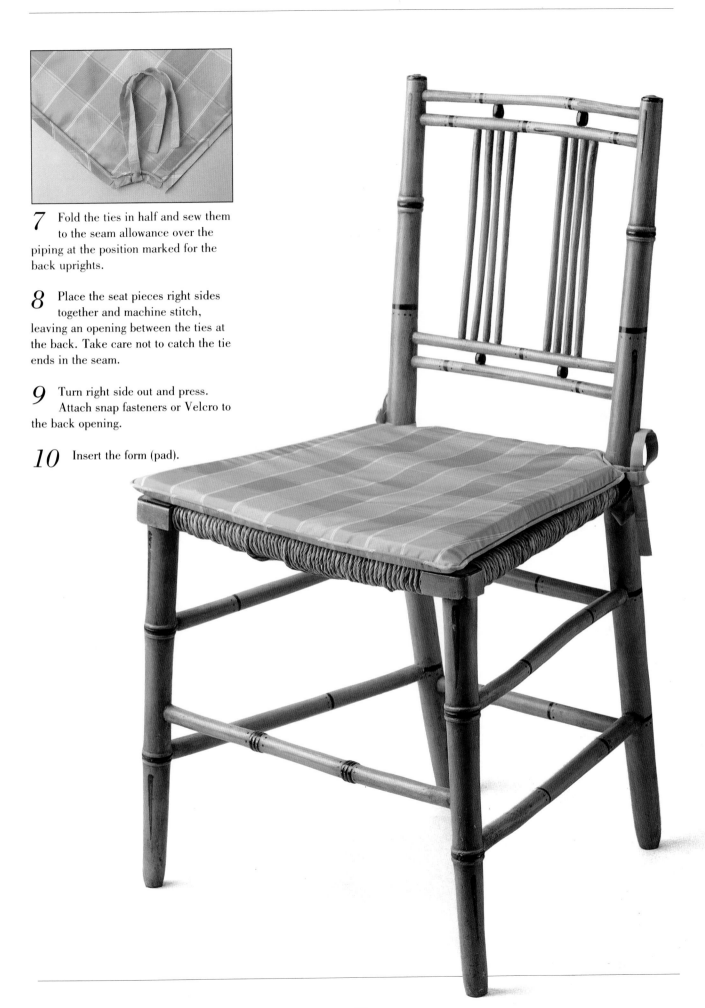

7 Fold the ties in half and sew them to the seam allowance over the piping at the position marked for the back uprights.

8 Place the seat pieces right sides together and machine stitch, leaving an opening between the ties at the back. Take care not to catch the tie ends in the seam.

9 Turn right side out and press. Attach snap fasteners or Velcro to the back opening.

10 Insert the form (pad).

CURTAINS

CURTAINS

*D*ressing the windows is probably the main soft furnishing project undertaken when decorating a room. It may be the style of window treatment or a particularly eye-catching fabric that is the point of inspiration for the whole room.

There are many things to consider before you start. You will need to decide whether you want the drapery to provide privacy or leave as much of the window uncovered as possible. You will have to make decisions about the style of the window treatment in keeping with the rest of the room, and whether the windows can be shown off to their best advantage with a certain type of drapery (see pages 150 to 158).

CHOOSING FABRIC

Fabric for curtains must have good draping qualities. You should never buy unless you have first seen the fabric draped, especially in the case of patterned fabric, as a pattern lying flat or on a

roll will look very different hanging. Always ask to see the fabric in daylight. Artificial light will alter the color considerably. Although curtains need quite a lot of fabric, always buy the best; this does not always mean the most expensive. A good fabric should have a straight weave with the pattern printed on the grain.

— CHOOSING RODS (TRACKS) —

Rods (tracks) are available in plastic and in metal, plastic rods (tracks) being more suitable for lightweight curtains, while heavy curtains are better hung from a metal traverse rod or ceiling track system. Most fixtures can be attached to the wall, to the window frame, or to the ceiling.

Curtains can also be hung from a pole. These are available in all types and shades of wood and also in brass. If there is to be a valance (pelmet), it is easier to combine a mounting board for these with a rod or ceiling track than it is with a pole.

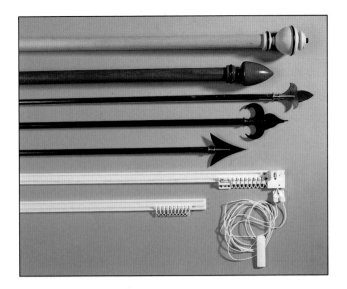

For heavy curtains and pale-colored fabrics, a cording system may be advisable. This is integrated with the traverse rod (track) and prevents putting strain or dirty fingers on the leading edge of the curtain.

Positioning Rods (Tracks) and Poles

Ideally curtains should be a further frame to the window. The positioning of the hardware changes the effect of the window treatment. For short curtains, the track or pole should be fixed as high above the window as the curtains are to hang below the windowsill.

With long drapery, the rod, track, or pole should be fixed midway between the ceiling and the top of the window. It should be at least 4 in (10 cm) above the window top – any lower and pools of light and heading tapes will show from the outside. The drapery should hang to the floor, or an extra 4–8 in (10–20 cm) may be added for a grander trailing effect.

In most cases the rod, track, or pole should extend either side of the window, enabling the curtains to be pulled well back and so allowing as much light as possible into the room. This will obviously not be possible in a recess. Special flexible rods (tracks) can be bent to fit in bay and bow windows.

It is good practice to attach the fixture before you calculate the fabric requirements.

Heading tapes are bought by the yard or meter, and they are attached to the top of the curtain fabric, then pulled up to form a range of headings – pleats, gathers, smocking or shirring. They are then attached to the rod, track, or pole by means of hooks. Headings can also be hand sewn for an individual finish. Detachable linings are also finished with a heading tape. The main types of tape include a standard heading tape, usually 1 in (2.5 cm) deep. This is suitable for use with small curtains and with lightweight fabrics. If this type is used, the length of the tape and the width of the fabric must be one-and-a-half to two-and-a-half times the length of the rod or track to allow for sufficient gathering.

Pencil pleat tape is suitable for most curtains hung from rods, tracks, or poles. It is gathered from two-and-a-half to three times the length of the fixture and gives a much fuller fabric cover to the window. Triple or pinch pleat tape is also 3 in (8 cm) deep and when pulled up it creates a pleat every 6 in (15 cm) or so.

Hand-sewn headings are made by placing interfacing at the top of the curtain and sewing pleats at regular intervals. This has to be calculated accurately (see page 35). The width of fabric must be at least two-and-a-quarter times the length of the rod or track.

MEASURING

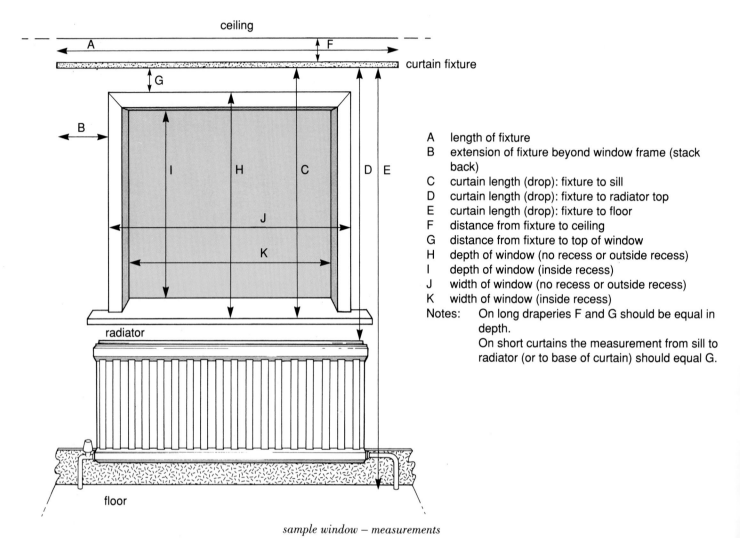

A   length of fixture
B   extension of fixture beyond window frame (stack back)
C   curtain length (drop): fixture to sill
D   curtain length (drop): fixture to radiator top
E   curtain length (drop): fixture to floor
F   distance from fixture to ceiling
G   distance from fixture to top of window
H   depth of window (no recess or outside recess)
I   depth of window (inside recess)
J   width of window (no recess or outside recess)
K   width of window (inside recess)
Notes: On long draperies F and G should be equal in depth.
          On short curtains the measurement from sill to radiator (or to base of curtain) should equal G.

sample window – measurements

The two measurements required for calculating the amount of fabric are the length of the rod or track plus any returns or overlaps, or of the pole to the finials, and the length or drop of the curtains.

The complete length of the support fixture should be measured and 4 in (10 cm) added to each side for the "return". Incorporating a return at each side will allow the curtain to fit flush to the wall, and will also hide the screws and fittings that secure the rod or track system. If two curtains are to be used, then an additional 3 in (8 cm) should be added for the overlap. If the curtains are to be hung from a pole, the pole length must

be measured, excluding the finials.

The drop measurement is determined by the type and style of heading used and whether the curtains are to be hung from a pole or from a rod or a ceiling track system. With standard heading tape, the drop is from the top of the rod or track. With pencil or pleated heading tape, the drop is from 1 in (2.5 cm) above the rod or track. When using a pole, the drop measurement is taken from the base of the ring. Depending on the style of window treatment, curtains should hang ½ in (12 mm) off the floor, or to the floor plus 4–6 in (10–15 cm). For curtains hanging in the window recess, allow ¼ in (6 mm) from the sill.

CALCULATING FABRIC REQUIREMENTS

When making drapes, allowances are needed for hems and turnings, 6 in (15 cm) for a double hem and a minimum of 2 in (5 cm) for the turn over at the top. These measurements are added to the length or drop. Measuring and calculating fabric quantities for swags and tails requires a different approach (see page 47).

Most furnishing fabrics are woven in one of the following widths:

48 in (122 cm),
54 in (137 cm),
and 60 in (152 cm).

So with the chosen curtain heading in mind, calculate how many widths of fabric, when joined together, will give a satisfactory fullness to the curtains.

Patterns printed on fabric are repeated evenly throughout the roll. These repeat measurements will be on the manufacturer's label, but you can measure them easily yourself. The most common repeats occur 6 in, 12½ in, or 25 in (15 cm, 32 cm or 64 cm) apart. When joining two widths of a patterned fabric, the pattern must be matched up. This is achieved by dividing the drop and hem and top allowance (drop plus 8 in/20 cm) measurement by the pattern repeat measurement, and rounding it up to a whole number of repeats. Each cut length must be made up of completed patterns. Each width cut will now be identical in pattern, so that the widths will match when they are joined together.

As the hem is the focal point of the curtain, it is a good idea to choose what part of the fabric will be at the bottom. It might be a particular color that you wish to bring out, or some part of the fabric might complement the carpet or wall color better than another. Generally, though, it is the pattern that will decide the hem line – it is far better to have a row of whole flowers or birds at the bottom edge of the curtain than a row of incomplete ones! To ensure that you can choose which part of the pattern will be at the bottom of the curtain, buy one extra pattern repeat per window.

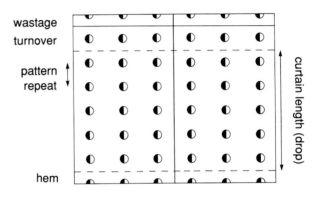

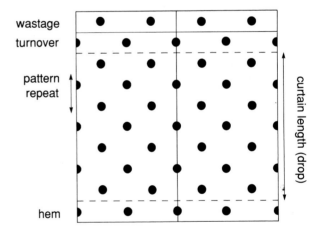

curtains made up of two widths of fabric – pattern repeat and half-drop pattern repeat

If you buy a fabric that has a half-drop pattern with an odd number of repeats across the fabric, an extra half pattern repeat is needed on each cut length. Remember to take this into your calculations. Any wastage can be cut off and used to make a valance (pelmet) or tiebacks.

bordered fabric

● seam

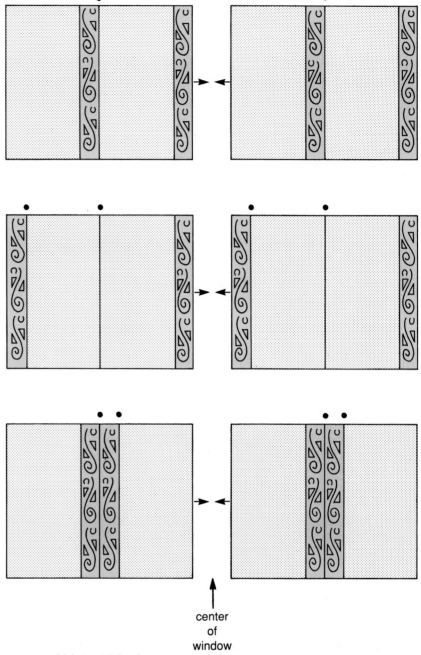

center
of
window

treatment of fabric with border pattern

Another pattern that requires thought when calculating and cutting out is one with a border, which may be down one side, or down both sides. These borders may be transferred from one side to the other, added to both sides, or removed from the middle where the widths join. There are all sorts of combinations: remember that any changes will alter the finished width of the curtain. Fabric with borders down both sides is better made up into narrower curtains, on small windows, for example, or in a bay.

Lace can be bought with pre-shaped borders that can be used either down the sides of a curtain or across the base and top for a decorative hem. When buying lace with either borders or a pattern, you need to make sure that any motifs are centrally placed and that any pre-cut edging rests just above the floor or windowsill (see page 57).

CURTAIN LININGS

Nearly all curtains look and handle better when they are lined and even better still when they are interlined as well. Linings protect the top fabric from dust, sunlight, and general wear. Put together with an interlining, they will provide good insulation and cut down on any drafts.

Produced in many colors and two standard widths – 48 in (122 cm) and 54 in (137 cm) – lining fabric is made of cotton sateen with one side that is slightly shiny. The traditional colors of white and cream are good to use with pale fabrics, and for those with a light background. Also, when used throughout the house, they give a uniform look to the outside of the building. Choose a good quality lining fabric without too much finish (dressing) or artificial stiffening, and one that does not crease easily. A more expensive option is to choose a plain or patterned chintz for the lining if you plan to tie the curtains back and make the lining a feature too.

There are blackout linings available, and these come in white and cream. They have a rubbery finish and are only suitable for use with dark heavy fabrics.

A curtain that is interlined will have a far more luxurious appearance, and will hang and drape better. Interlining is a thick fluffy fabric made either from cotton waste or from synthetic fibers. It is cut to the same size as the top fabric, and then made up with it as one. Of the two types, the synthetic version is by far the better; it handles well, stays where it is put, and gives the curtains a well-made and professional look. The cotton type, known as linterfelt (bump), is slightly thicker and does give draperies a heavier and perhaps grander appearance, but it is much more difficult to handle, having a looser weave so that it moves and stretches more readily. It also produces vast amounts of fluff while you work and does not always clean successfully.

In a room where most of the furnishings are made from natural fibers, it is unlikely that having a synthetic interlining to the curtains will cause any condensation problems.

Obviously, when estimating the amount of lining fabric there are no patterns to match up, so the quantities are the same as for a plain top fabric – curtain length (drop) plus hems and turnings multiplied by the number of widths.

MAKING UNLINED CURTAINS

Curtains without linings are best kept for small windows where bulk would be a problem, and for curtains in a fabric designed to float and billow. These curtains are machine stitched with all raw edges hidden. Loose-lined curtains are machine stitched in the same way and have a lining made up separately, attached to the curtain with a special tape (see page 37). The lining may then be cleaned more frequently than the more delicate top fabric.

Materials

rod, ceiling track, or pole and rings, secured in position
chosen heading tape with hooks
curtain fabric
yardstick (meter ruler)*
sharp scissors
soft pencil

* A wooden yardstick or meter ruler is useful, not just for accurate measurements, but also for smoothing fabric that is out of arms' reach.

1 Use the largest flat area available. Make sure from the start that your fabric is cut straight and that the pattern is printed on the grain line, or weft thread – that is the thread going across the fabric. It is the grain line that the cutting must follow. Decide on your hem line and make your cut 6 in (15 cm) below this. Now cut all your lengths of fabric one after the other.

If several lengths are to be cut, you may find it easier to mark all the measurements on to a pole and use this as a yardstick, marking both sides of the fabric to these measurements before cutting. The same pole may then be used for cutting out the lining and interlining (if using).

2 To join two widths, with right side facing up, place the selvages of the two lengths together. Fold and press one side under to include up to a maximum of 1 in (2.5 cm) of the pattern. Place this onto the other length of fabric, matching up the pattern as you pin the two pieces together. Put the pins on the more prominent pattern markings (see page 32).

3 Fold the top length over so that the fabric is lying right sides together, and pin the selvages together. Remove the pins that were keeping the pattern matched and smooth out the two lengths. Pin the two pieces together at intervals, in a line approximately 10 in (25 cm) from the selvage.

4 Machine stitch down the crease line using a small stitch.

5 Cut one selvage narrower than the other, and stitch a flat-fell seam.

6 Press the front of the fabric along the stitched seam using the point of the iron.

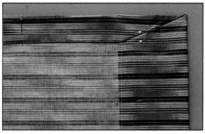

7 Fold and pin the side seams in by 1½ in (4 cm) with the raw edges folded under by ½ in (12 mm). Form the mitered corner (see page 33), and when the hem and all seams are folded, pinned, and pressed, machine stitch along the top of the fold.

8 Make sure the fabric is straight across the top edge, turn over a 2 in (5 cm) allowance, and secure with pins. Measure up for the curtain tape, and cut a length plus 1 in (2.5 cm) turning allowance.

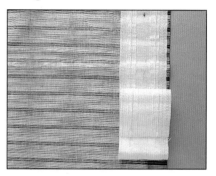

9 Pin the heading tape in place across the top edge of the curtain, turning under ½ in (12 mm) at either end. All raw edges should be covered. Keeping the tape taut, machine with a line of stitching ¼ in (6 mm) from the top. Remove the pins and pin the bottom of the tape to the curtain, making sure the row of hook pockets are vertically in line. Sew the second row of stitches along the base of the tape and on the sides, leaving a gap in the middle of each side.

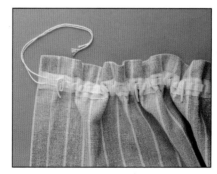

10 Pull the cords up from each end of the heading tape to the required length to fit the curtain rod or track, and tie them firmly.

11 Fit the hooks into the loops and hang the curtains.

LINED CURTAINS

*L*ined and interlined draperies are a worthwhile investment of your time. They hang well and last a long time. They also provide valuable insulation at night in winter.

Materials

curtain fabric
lining fabric in neutral or co-
ordinating color
interlining
heading tape and hooks
two strips of cardboard, both
16 in (40 cm) long – one 2 in
(5 cm) wide, the other 3 in (8 cm)
wide*

* These are useful for making
smooth and accurate side seams
and hems.

---

1 Use the largest flat area available. Make sure from the start that your fabric is cut straight and that the pattern is printed on the grain line, or weft thread – that is the thread going across the fabric. It is the grain line that the cutting must follow. Decide on your hem line and make your cut 6 in (15 cm) below this. Now cut all your lengths of fabric one after the other.

If several lengths are to be cut, you may find it easier to mark all the measurements on to a pole and use this as a yardstick, marking both sides of the fabric to these measurements before cutting. Having a pole marked out saves time and worry over making mistakes with your measurements. Having cut out the top fabric, the same pole may then be used for cutting out the lining and interlining (see below).

2 To join two widths, with right side facing up, place the selvages of the two lengths together, fold and press one side in to include up to a maximum of 1 in (2.5 cm) of the pattern. Place this onto the other length of fabric, matching up the pattern as you pin the two pieces together. Put the pins on the more prominent pattern markings, such as where a flower stem crosses the join.

3 Fold the top length over so the fabric is lying right sides together, and pin the selvages together. Remove the pins that were keeping the pattern matched and smooth out the two lengths. Pin the two pieces together at intervals, in a line approximately 10 in (25 cm) from the selvage.

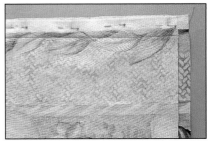

4 Machine stitch down the crease line using a small stitch.

5 Cut off all the selvages. These are woven more tightly, and will pucker the seam if left. Also, being devoid of pattern and color, they can sometimes show through to the front of the curtain in certain lights.

6 Calculate and cut out the pieces for the lining fabric. The total width of lining fabric should be 3 in (8 cm) narrower and 2 in (5 cm) shorter than the main fabric. When joining lining widths together, make sure that you use the shiny side as the right side. Snip the selvage along the edge about every 10 in (20 cm) to release the tension.

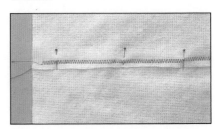

7 Cut out the widths of interlining. Because it is a fabric with a loose weave, it is best joined by overlapping the two pieces, and then sewing them with a zigzag stitch to reduce bulk. Pin the pieces together before sewing so the fabric does not stretch.

8 Press open all seams on the curtain and lining.

9 Lay the main fabric face down on the table and place the interlining on top of it, smoothing it out well.

10 Trim the interlining to exactly the same size as the main fabric and smooth again. The two fabrics will cling together and from now on may be treated as one.

11 Mark what is to be the top of the curtain with pins or a pencil mark. Draw pencil lines down the length of the fabric, 1½ in (4 cm) from each side edge.

12 Stitch the main fabric and interlining together down these lines, using a large backstitch. The sewing thread should only catch two to three threads of the main fabric, and therefore be almost invisible at the front. This will keep the edge of the curtain well padded. The interlining must also be attached to the main fabric over the whole width of the curtain. Having backstitched each side, sew a line of lockstitch (a blanket stitch 8–12 in/20–30 cm long as shown) down every half width of fabric.

13 Fold in the side seam by 2 in (5 cm) using the cardboard, pushing it into the fold. Remove the cardboard and pin the seam in place.

14 Fold over the hem by 3 in (8 cm) using the cardboard, then by another 3 in (8 cm), pushing the cardboard into the fold. Slide it along as you pin the doubled hem.

15 To form the mitered corner, press creases where the hems are pinned, and then open up the side seam by 12 in (30 cm), where the double hem meets the edge of the fabric, and mark a 1. Open up one fold of the hem by 12 in (30 cm), and where the crease of the side seam meets the single hem, mark a 2. Fold back the side seam over the single hem, and where the side seam meets the bottom of the single hem, mark a 3. Now open up the side seam again, and check that marks 1, 2, and 3 form a diagonal line. Fold this over and press well.

16 Fold in the side seam and fold up the hem by the second fold, and pin into place. Finish the other side of the curtain in exactly the same way.

17 Hand sew the side seams using a large backstitch 1¼ in (3 cm) in from the curtain edge. These will be covered by the lining fabric. The stitch used for the hem should be loose and with the thread well hidden in the fold. Sew the miter together, using a ladder stitch, pulling it tight from the top, and closing the join up neatly.

18 To fit the lining, fold up the hem of the lining twice to form a 3 in (8 cm) double hem. Pin the hem in place and machine stitch along the top of the fold. (Short curtains may have a 2 in/5 cm double hem.)

19 Mark the center lines of the curtain and the lining from the top to the bottom of the fabrics. Lay the curtain on the table with the wrong side up. Lay the lining on top of the curtain with the right side up. Pin the two together down the center line, with the lining hem finishing 2 in (5 cm) above the curtain hem.

20 Fold the lining back to fall right sides together, and lockstitch between the fabric/ interlining and the lining. Do this every half width of fabric, pinning the lining hem 2 in (5 cm) above the curtain hem all the way along until the mitered corners are reached.

21 When you reach the corners 1 in (2.5 cm) from the sides of the curtain, turn under the sides of the lining and trim off any excess. Then smooth it out and pin it into place. The weave of the lining fabric is not always straight, so you will probably find that there is an uneven amount of lining fabric to trim off between the top and bottom of the curtain, and it is for this reason that the middle of the curtain is used as the starting point.

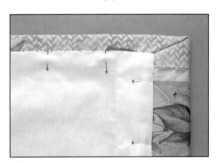

22 Hand sew the lining to the curtain fabric using a catch stitch down the side seams, hiding the thread in between the layers of fabric. The hem is left loose, except at the half width marks, where it is held by the lockstitch.

23 With the curtain lining in place, smooth out the curtain to make sure that there are no gathers, tucks, or creases in the fabrics. Insert a row of pins, positioned vertically, along the width of the lining hem, to keep the top fabric and the lining together. Then insert another row of pins 10 in (25 cm) from the top of the curtain.

24 Measure out and mark the length (drop measurement) from the curtain hem upwards at intervals along the curtain width, and draw a line through these in pencil. Then fold over the lining, interlining, and top fabric along this line, and pin them down. Leave 2–4 in (5–10 cm) of fabric below this top fold, and trim off any excess.

25 Now pin and machine stitch the heading tape as for unlined curtains (see page 31, steps 8 and 9).

26 Pull the cords up from both sides until the curtain top measures the same as the length of rod or track it is to cover, not forgetting to make allowances for any returns or overlaps. Tie off the cords, wind them up, and push them between the tape and the fabric. Doing this rather than using a cord tidy helps to keep the edges firm and makes the overlap more effective.

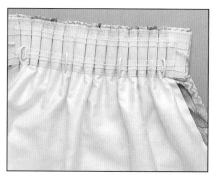

27 Place the appropriate hooks in the correct pockets at regular intervals of 4–8 in (10–20 cm).

HAND SEWN HEADINGS

*H*and sewn headings have several advantages over taped headings. The pleats and gathers are fixed, unlike tapes that sometimes move; the finished curtains stack back farther, and will have a more tailored appearance; any pattern can be incorporated into the heading (vertical stripes, for example); and there will be no machine stitching showing on the front of the curtain.

Materials

interlined and lined curtain (see page 32) up to step 24*
5 in (13 cm) wide iron-on heading buckram
metal tape measure

* See step 1 below.

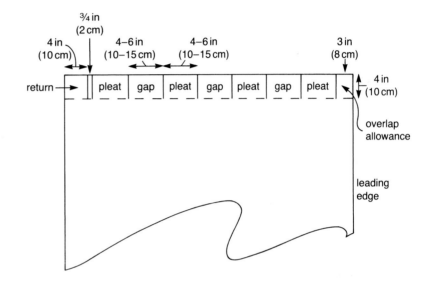

hand sewn headings – pleat calculation

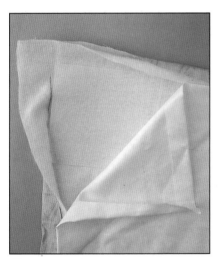

1 Prepare the curtains up to step 24 except that after drawing the line marking the length (drop) measurement, fold back the top of the lining, and insert the heading buckram beneath it, keeping the top level with the pencil line, and the sides pushed well into the side seams.

2 Fold over the top fabric and interlining, and press the turnover and side seams – all the top fabric that is showing – so that the adhesive in the heading buckram keeps everything in place while you position the lining.

3 Bring the lining back up to cover the heading buckram, turning under its raw edge by ½ in (12 mm) from the top of the curtain. Press the top of the lining, making sure that there are no creases in the fabric, as this will stick to the buckram. Finish by slipstitching together along the top of the side seams and the top of the lining.

4 To calculate for the pleats, lay the curtain flat on the table with the lining side up, and measure the top from edge to edge using a metal tape measure. On each side, mark a line from the top of the curtain to the bottom of the heading buckram. This should be 4 in (10 cm) in on the side with the return, and 3 in (8 cm) in on the side that is to be the leading edge, for the overlap.

5 The length between these two marks is divided into the pleats and gaps between these pleats. Each pleat needs approximately 6 in (15 cm) of fabric (or 4 in/10 cm in the case of cartridge pleats), and each gap must have between 4–6 in (10–15 cm) of fabric. There is always one more pleat than gap, and the gap measurements must add up to the length of rod or track that they are to cover. Therefore divide this length by 4½–5 in (12–13 cm) to find the number of gaps that will be required. If the curtain is a bit wide for the rail, put extra fabric into the pleats, and if it is a bit small, put in less fabric. Start the first pleat ¾ in (2 cm) in from the return; this prevents the pleat from splaying out on the corner.
The diagram above shows how the curtain would be marked.

6 With the back of the curtain marked out, pin the sides of the pleats together. Taking care to keep the tops together, machine stitch down the pair of parallel pencil lines that form each pleat, from the top to the bottom of the buckram.

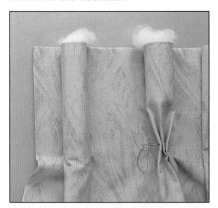

7 To form organ pleats, use 4 in (10 cm) of fabric. Pad the pleat with batting (wadding), so that it resembles a cylinder.

8 To form cartridge pleats, make as for organ pleats, but gather at the base and pad as before.

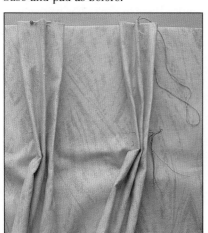

9 To form pinch or French pleats, use 6 in (15 cm) of fabric. Divide the pleat into three equal small pleats, oversew together at the top, and stab stitch through all layers at the base.

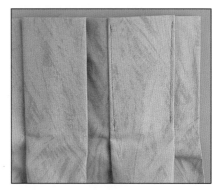

10 To make box pleats, use 6 in (15 cm) of fabric, and press flat to form pleats. Machine or hand stitch on either side of each pleat.

11 Remove all the pins from the curtain. With the exception of the edges of interlined curtains, press well on both the front and the back, trying to keep the rounded appearance of the edges.

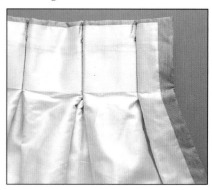

12 Using the appropriate hooks, attach one to the back of each pleat and hang the curtains from the rod or track.

13 Pull the curtains back, and drape the gathers evenly. Hold the draping in place by using fabric ties around them at intervals down the curtain, and leave these for a few days to train the pleats.

LOOSE LINED CURTAINS

*L*oose linings are attached to the main curtains by means of a special heading tape to which the hooks are attached before being inserted through the curtain heading tape. They can be easily removed for laundering. Although they will not improve the way the curtains hang, they do provide extra insulation, and protect the main fabric from fading in the sun.

> **Materials**
>
> unlined curtains (see page 31)
> lining fabric
> special lining heading tape

1 Measure the width of the unlined curtains and make up the lining (see page 32), so that with side hems it measures 2 in (5 cm) narrower than this. The hem should lie 2 in (5 cm) above the curtain hem. Turn in ½ in (12 mm) and then 1½ in (4 cm) down both sides and across the bottom, and machine stitch.

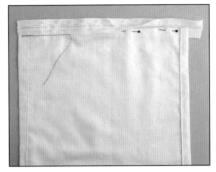

2 Check that the raw edge of the top of the lining aligns with hook pockets on the curtain heading tape. Cut off any excess if necessary. Slip the raw edge between the two layers of heading tape, and machine stitch around all edges.

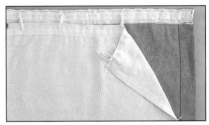

3 After pulling up the cords on lining and curtain heading tapes to fit the rod (track), insert the hooks through the lining, and then through the curtain.

4 If necessary, hand sew the occasional string of chain stitches between the lining and the top of the fabric down the side edges.

INDIVIDUAL TOUCHES

As well as basic curtain headings, there are several possible alternatives and variations with similar themes that, with different edgings, can give your curtains a style of their own. Smocking makes an attractive heading; this can be achieved with a tape, and may be further embroidered, or can be completely hand sewn. Choose a fairly plain curtain fabric, otherwise the smocked pattern will be lost.

Hand-sewn headings can have buttons, rosettes, and cords attached to them. Ruffles falling from the top of the curtain look carefree and relaxed. If the fabric is heavy, the ruffle or frill will pull down and expose the hooks, so it is advisable to catch the fabric to the rings.

A simple touch is to add a contrasting binding to the top of the curtain or even around all four edges. Sew the tape on following the join of the two fabrics. (Then only one line of machine stitching will be noticeable.)

EDGES AND BORDERS

Fringes and cords of all shapes and sizes can be hand sewn to the sides of curtains, but unless the draperies are designed to be seen drawn against an expanse of wall, the trimming is usually only on the leading edge. A bullion fringe looks good on a hem that sweeps the floor.

Borders and contrasting edges should be sewn in place before the curtains are made up. Remember to miter the corners (see page 33), because the joins will be seen from the front.

Ruffles (frills), pleats, and piping all have their place as curtain edgings, and should be made up first. Ruffles (frills) require fabric twice the length to be covered, and pleats three times. Hide any joins in the folds of the fabric. Always use similar quality fabrics for both the main fabrics and the edgings.

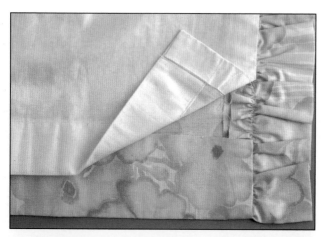

To add ruffles (frills), pleats, and piping to the curtain edge, pin and then sew the ruffle (frill) to the side seam as the curtains are being made up. The ruffle (frill) should go right to the top, not stop at the bottom of the tape. There is no need for a miter on the hem, as all raw seams are covered by the lining, which is brought right up to the ruffle (frill).

Making Piping

To make piping, it is necessary to cut out and make up bias strips (see page 122).

Piping can be made flat without a filling or with cord, which can be bought in many thicknesses. The choice of thickness depends on the style. Heavy rope-like piping would suit a baroque-style interior with heavyweight upholstery fabrics. Cotton and chintz fabrics look better with piping in narrower widths.

Cut the bias strips to double the width of the cord plus seam allowance. Wrap the bias strip around the cord and align the raw edges, pinning at regular intervals. Using the zipper foot on your machine, it is a simple matter when the piping is *in situ* to machine stitch the strip. Place the stitching a little way away from the cord, so that when it is inserted in position on the curtain, the final stitching can be done closer to the cord, thereby covering the initial stitches.

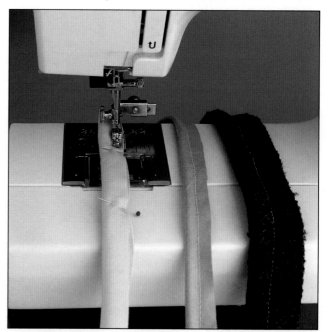

VALANCES AND PELMETS

Valances and pelmets grace the top of the window, hiding the curtain fixtures, and they can make a significant difference to the design of the room, particularly to the window treatment. In the United States a top treatment can be called cornice, but a general term is valance. In Europe pelmets have a stiffened base and valances are generally frilled or pleated.

Stiffened valances (pelmets) such as the one above are more formal. They are usually made from pelmet buckram, then covered with interlining, and a top fabric, which can be decorated with braids, fringes, or tassels. The pelmet buckram can be cut to any shape, although sharp angles are difficult to cover and sometimes require a braid to hide any raw edges that may show on the front. A lining should be sewn to the back of the valance (pelmet).

Some valances (pelmets) have extended sides and are more elaborate. These are known as cornices or lambrequins, and if particularly large are better mounted on a wooden base.

Valances can be made in a similar style to any curtain heading, whether taped or handsewn. If the matching curtains are interlined, then the valance should be too. The valance should also match the fullness of the curtains but try to avoid having a seam down the middle. It may have scalloped edges, but it is advisable to follow the line of the window frame or the width of the curtains when drawn back in the daytime.

The length or drop measurement of valances (pelmets) should be at least 10 per cent of the curtain length and, in all but small cottage windows, preferably more.

Valances (pelmets) are hung from rods (tracks) that are mounted in front of the curtain rod. They can also be attached to mounting boards either with Velcro glued to the board and stitched on the fabric, or with staples or small upholstery tacks. The board is made up rather like a shelf above the window. It should be secured to angle irons that are screwed into the wall above the window or directly into the frame – this depends on the style. The top of the mounting (pelmet) board can be painted to match the wall, or covered with matching fabric.

varying lengths of valance (pelmet) according to window and draperies

MAKING A VALANCE

Materials

curtain fabric*
contrasting edging if required
lining fabric and interlining
heading tape and hooks
valance rod (track) or mounting board secured above the curtain rod

* The valance should be the same width as the curtains. If it is covering a blind, the choice of heading tape will determine the width.

1 Decide on the depth of the valance. You can either cut out a paper pattern, or hang a piece of fabric from the valance board, and stand back to gauge the effect. Try to cover all the top part of the window frame. Now check the proportions: would the window be better with even more glass covered, or should the hem of the valance be shaped in some way, higher in the center than at the sides, or with scallops, zigzags, or a ruffle (frill)?

2 Add 1 in (2.5 cm) for a turnover at the top and 1 in (2.5 cm) seam allowance at the bottom and on both sides. Cut the lining out to the same measurements but 1 in (2.5 cm) shorter and 2 in (5 cm) narrower. Cut out and

attach the interlining to the curtain fabric, if any.

3 With right sides together, machine stitch the lining and curtain fabric together down both sides ½ in (12 mm) from the raw edges, and press, so that the curtain fabric forms two even borders at each end.

4 Machine stitch the curtain fabric and lining together along the base (hem). Turn right side out and press again.

5 Turn down the allowance at the top and sew on the heading tape in the same way as for curtains (see page 31).

6 Pull up the cords to fit the window, and either fix the valance to the curtain rod (track) with hooks as for curtains, or tack it to the front of the mounting (pelmet) board. Alternatively, sew pieces of Velcro along the top of the valance through the heading tape (after gathering it up), and glue or staple the other strips to the leading edge of the board.

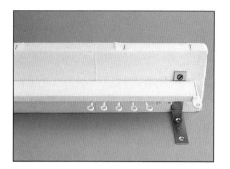

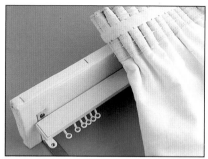

Decorative Edgings

Pick out one of the colors in a patterned fabric and use to add a strip to the edge of the valance (pelmet).

To make a bound edge, add a strip of bias-cut fabric (see page 122) in a contrasting color to the base of the main fabric at step 2.

To calculate the amount of binding, make up a piece of bias the length of the hem to be bound plus 1 in (2.5 cm) and the width of the finished binding doubled and allowing 1 in (2.5 cm) seam allowance. For a bold valance, the binding should be about 1 in (2.5 cm) wide to make enough of a visual impact.

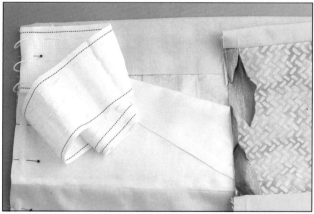

To attach the binding, make up a strip long enough and press. With right sides together, pin the binding along the valance edge and machine stitch, leaving a ½ in (12 mm) seam allowance. Trim the excess fabric and turn the binding to the wrong side, turning back evenly, so the required amount of binding is showing all along the hem. Machine stitch the lining to this as described in step 3 above.

To Make a Shaped Edge

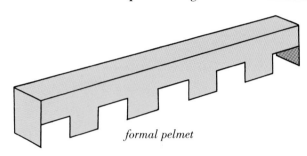

formal pelmet

Plan the edge and make up a paper pattern. Work as for the valance up to step 2 but with right sides together and the lining the same size as the main fabric, machine stitch along both sides and along the hem, incorporating the design, whether zigzags or scallops.

Clip the seams and turn right side out. Press the hem well so the lining fabric does not show through on the right side.

A valance with a shaped edge should not have too tight a heading as this will need too much fabric and the shapes will be lost in the folds of fabric when the valance is hung.

TIEBACKS

*T*iebacks can add style, flair, and color to the window treatment as well as having the practical task of holding the curtains securely and away from the glass.

Positioning and size can alter the whole style of the window treatment. On long, full-length draperies, the tieback is usually hooked up at the midpoint, but can be hung higher or lower to give a quite different effect.

A small, tight tieback will give the curtains a sharp and tailored look, whereas a large, loose tieback will allow the curtains to lie in soft drapes. With short curtains, tiebacks should only be a part of an informally dressed window. On cottage-style windows, however, cords or simple bows would be more suitable. A formal tieback on a short formal curtain can set the whole window treatment out of proportion and is often overpowering.

The classic tieback is crescent-shaped and stiffened with pelmet buckram. It may be edged with cording or piping, ruffles (frills), or pleats and decorated with bows, rosettes, or fringes. It can be made from the same fabric as the curtains or with a plain fabric of a color picked from the main curtain fabric.

Straight tiebacks and those made with a softer base can be just as formal. Alternative possibilities for tiebacks include bows, tubes, and cords. Large, floppy bows with long tails are attractive and simple. These are made up with the bows sewn permanently into place; the bow would become very creased if it were to be tied and retied again and again.

A rosette is a flamboyant alternative to a tieback. Cut a length of fabric to double the width of the diameter of the finished rosette plus 1 in (2.5 cm) allowance and as long as the circumference. The size will depend on the curtain style. Join the two short edges together to make a circle of fabric and fold in half lengthwise with wrong sides together. Run a gathering thread ½ in (12 mm) from the raw edges and pull up to

form a rosette. Secure firmly, and cover the raw edges with a covered button or other decorative motif. A "chou" is a larger, softer version of a rosette.

Padded tubes, either smooth or ruched, may be used, or three tubes can be braided (plaited) together, in colors chosen to complement the curtains or in one matching or contrasting color. For padded tubes, choose a fabric that is soft enough to bend easily, yet sufficiently thick to pad out the creases in the batting (wadding). Cord tiebacks can suit every style made in cotton and in silk, plain colored and multi-colored, and with tassels in various degrees of splendor.

Wall hooks, to which the tiebacks will attach, are available in designs to suit all styles of room.

An alternative to tiebacks and hooks are "holdbacks". These are large, brass rosettes or decorated clips that are fixed to the wall, slightly set back from the window; the curtain is tucked behind them. These have the advantage of being quick to use, and are less likely to crease the curtain.

MEASURING FOR TIEBACKS

To calculate the length of a tieback, pass a cloth tape measure around the curtain and, holding it against the wall, drape the curtains to suit the window. This will give you the best length for most tiebacks, though a braided (plaited) style will require an additional 10 per cent.

STIFFENED TIEBACKS

Materials

paper for template	lining fabric
heavyweight buckram	small rings (two per tieback)
interlining: polyester batting	
main fabric*	
piping in a contrasting color (see page 38)	* Tiebacks are usually cut from the wastage of the curtain lengths but try to place them carefully.
fabric adhesive	

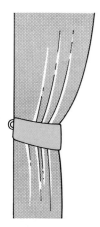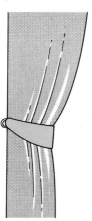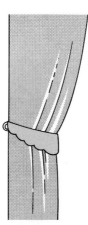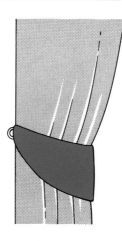

different tieback shapes

1 Cut out a paper template to the shape and size required. The diagram above shows some possibilities.

2 Using the template, cut out the interfacing.

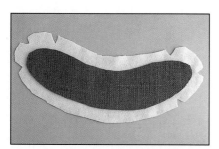

3 Cover one side of the pelmet buckram with interlining, cutting it 1½ in (4 cm) larger than the interfacing all the way around, so that it can be folded over at the edges.

When in place, the interlining will adhere to the stiffened buckram.

4 Cut out the top fabric, 1½ in (4 cm) larger than the template. Make sure that the fabric is cut on the straight of the grain.

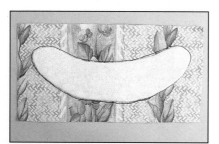

5 With the top fabric face up, lay the stiffened buckram, now covered with interlining, onto the top fabric and draw around it, sloping the pencil away to give a generous outline.

6 Machine stitch the piping or other decoration onto this line, making sure that all the rough edges are facing the same way and, where possible, positioning the join in the piping out of sight at the back of the tiebacks.

7 Glue the fabric to the overlapping interlining at the back of the tieback interfacing and trim off any excess. The piping should sit on the edge of the tieback.

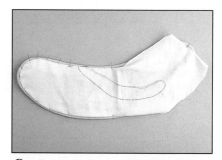

8 Cover the back with lining fabric, pinning it on from the middle, and working outwards. Then turn the rough edges in and handsew to the piping.

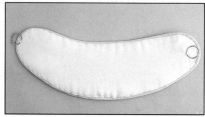

9 Sew two small rings to the ends of each tieback, the front one set back and concealed, the back one on the end and more prominent.

A TUBED AND RUCHED TIEBACK

Materials

main fabric
interlining
lightweight fiberfill batting
(terylene wadding)
length of cord
rings

1 Cut the fabric and the interlining to the measured length plus 1 in (2.5 cm) for the smooth-tubed tieback and twice the measured length plus 1 in (2.5 cm) for the ruched tieback, and cut both 11 in (28 cm) wide.

2 Lay the fabric face down with the interlining on top and, for the tubed tieback, spread a layer of loose fiberfill batting (terylene wadding) down its length. Use the same amount for the ruched tieback, but spread it more thinly over the whole length.

3 For ruched tiebacks, attach a cord firmly to one end of the length of fabric, and lay it along the full length on top of the batting (wadding), so that it extends beyond the other end.

4 Fold the fabric and interlining over and around the batting (wadding) and, allowing ½ in (12 mm) for the seams, pin the two sides together before hand sewing with very small stitches.

5 Pull the cord up on the ruched tieback, gathering the fabric and padding until it reaches the measured length, then fasten the cord off firmly.

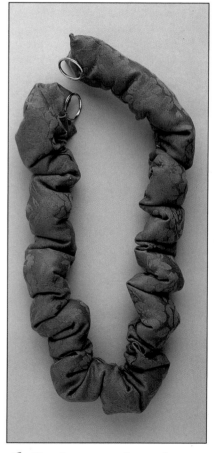

6 Turn in any raw edges and slipstitch to finish the ends, sewing a ring to each end as on page 44.

BRAIDED (PLAITED) TIEBACK

Materials

main fabric*
interlining
rings

* Use different colors in the
same fabric as the curtain.

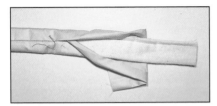

1 Cut the fabric and interlining to
the measured length (plus 10 per
cent for the braiding/plaiting) and
6½ in (16 cm) wide. Lay the top fabric
face down with the interlining on top.
Fold the fabric over lengthwise to form
a tube and, allowing ½ in (12 mm)
each side for seams, pin and slipstitch
into place. There is no need to turn in
the ends.

2 Make up three tubes in fabrics
and colors to suit the curtains.

3 Place one end of all the tubes
together, and whipstitch (oversew)
firmly. Now braid (plait) them, keeping
the seams of the tubes hidden. Fasten
off the other ends in a similar fashion.

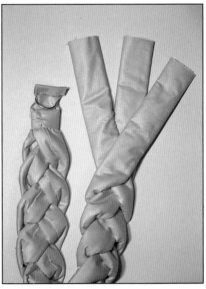

4 Cut two small pieces of fabric 3 in
(8 cm) long and 2 in (5 cm) wide.
Press in a ¼ in (6 mm) seam all the
way around. Pin one of these on each
end of the braiding (plaiting) and fold
it over to cover all the rough edges.
Sew in place.

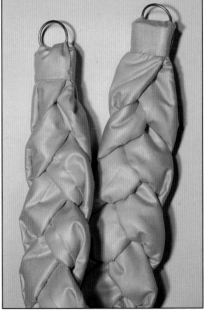

5 Sew a ring to each end as
described on page 44.

SWAGS AND TAILS

S wags and tails consist of softly draping fabrics which frame the top of the window, hanging over the curtains. Swags should be at least one fifth of the curtain's length, and tails between one third and one half. The number of swags depends on the size of the window and should, where appropriate, correspond to the layout of the window frame. Each swag overlaps its neighbor slightly.

The tails frame each side of the window with parallel folds increasing in length toward the curtain edge. Smaller, more open tails can be placed between the swags. Swags and tails are either tacked or stapled to a mounting (pelmet) board (see page 41) which is fixed with angle brackets above the curtain. Deep swags will keep out light from the room unless the board is hung well above the window, but remember that unless the curtains are hung high too, there is a risk that the curtain heading will show at the angles between the swags. The board should be at least 4–6 in (10–15 cm) wide to allow the curtains to pass freely below, and so as not to distort the lines

of the tails when drawn back. Cover the board with lining fabric.

Swags and tails made with furnishing fabric and a lining will have a sharp, tailored look, while adding an interlining will give the draping and pleating a softer, more rounded appearance. Fine, loosely woven fabrics drape and pleat well without interlining. Choose the lining carefully as it will show, particularly in the folds of the tails, as well as from the outside. The lining should be of a slightly finer fabric than the top fabric. If it is darker in color, use an interlining to prevent the stronger color showing through (test for this with the daylight shining behind).

All fabrics drape better when cut on the bias (across the weave), so swags should be cut in this way. If you are thinking of using a patterned fabric, you must therefore consider whether your pattern will still be attractive if it is hung at an angle. Will it still look good with the curtains? If not, choose a contrasting, plain color for both the top fabric and the lining, and perhaps use the patterned fabric on the tails alone.

MAKING SWAGS AND TAILS

There are many ways of making swags and tails but by using the methods described here and on the next two pages you should be able to create a good effect. It might be worth trying out the designs on a small window first to gain experience of the techniques.

Materials

fabric and lining in chosen colors and/or patterns
interlining if needed
mounting (pelmet) board
paper for template
staples or tacks to secure

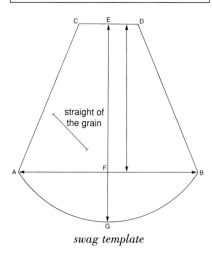

swag template

1 Decide how many swags you are to have and how long they are to be. Then work out how wide each swag will be and add 2 in (5 cm) to each to allow for the overlap. Cut paper templates so that the width along the top is half that of the finished swag and overlap (CD), and then gradually increases so that the width three-quarters of the way down (AB) is one-and-a-half times that of the finished width. The lower quarter of the template forms the curve of the swag.

The template length (EG) should be two-and-a-half times the desired length of the finished swag. EF is ¾ EG.

2 Cut out two identical templates and draw a line down the center front of each of them.

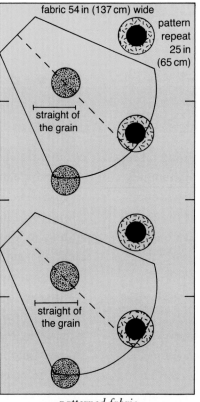

patterned fabric

3 If one of the chosen fabrics is patterned, lay one template across the fabric, marking the straight grain line of the fabric on the template, and choosing a suitable part of the pattern to be the center and base curve. Then lay the other template on the fabric along the same lines and pattern markings as the first, and continue in this way until you have cut out the number required.

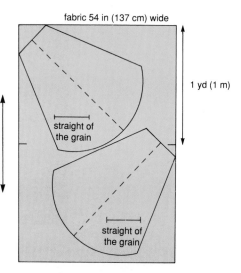

plain fabric

4 For plain fabrics and linings, lay the first template across the fabric, marking the straight grain as before. This time, the second template may be placed at a reversed angle (still keeping the grain line straight); better use can be made of the fabric this way. Cut out as many as you need.

5 Cut out the interlining using the same template, one per swag. As interlining is a loosely woven fabric it does not need to be cut on the bias.

6 Layer the three fabrics together; interlining first, then the top fabric (face up), and finally the lining fabric face down on the top.

7 Pin together all around and machine stitch the base curve only.

8 Unpin and rearrange the layers, so that the top and lining fabrics are right side out and the interlining is

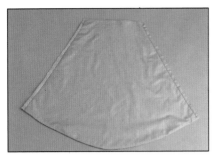

sandwiched in between. Press the seam carefully. Now pin the layers together again, and machine stitch them down both sides and along the top. The swag is now ready to be pleated.

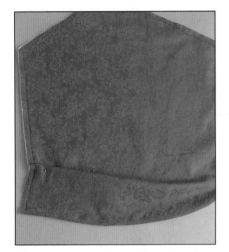

9 Mark out on the work surface the finished width of each swag and the center of this measurement. Then, on the fabric, mark the center of the top of the swag and place the two center marks together. Bring up the bottom corners of the swag to meet the two points at each end of the finished width on the rule.

10 Keeping these three points fixed, pleat up the swag in drapes and folds to suit your room and window treatment. Normally there is a flat piece in the middle with pleats radiating out towards the sides – a small one first with the pleats becoming progressively larger. Pin the pleating firmly in place.

11 Make up all the swags to look as similar as possible.

12 Cut strips of fabric to the same width as the finished swag and 4 in (10 cm) long. Place these strips face down along the top of the swag, over the pleats, and machine stitch carefully as the fabric will be bulky.

13 The swags are now ready for hanging. Use the strips of fabric sewn to them to staple or tack each swag to the top surface of the board.

MAKING TAILS

*T*ails hang on top of swags and usually frame them. Decide first how wide your tails are to be and how much of the swag they are to cover. The length should either be a half to a third of the curtain drop, or down perhaps to a dado molding or a particular point on the window frame.

Tails, like swags, are made with layers of fabric but this time they can be cut on the straight grain of the fabric. The formula for the template for the tail width is as follows: number of pleats × width of fold × 3 + 1 width of fold + distance of return to wall (the width of the board).

The tails are cut with the inner edge shorter than the outer edge, the inner being one quarter the length of the outer. The diagonal line between the short and long sides may be curved or straight; a curved line will allow more of the lining fabric to show on the pleats.

Materials

main fabric	paper for template
lining	mounting (pelmet) board
interlining if needed	staples or tacks to secure

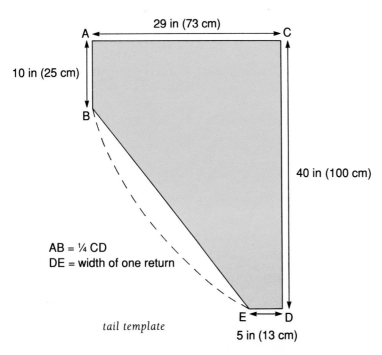

A — 29 in (73 cm) → C

10 in (25 cm)

B

40 in (100 cm)

AB = ¼ CD
DE = width of one return

E — D

tail template

5 in (13 cm)

4 Turn right side out, and press the edges down well.

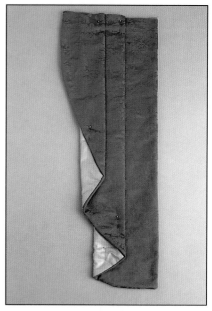

1 Cut out two identical templates and lay them on the fabric following the straight grain.

2 If using patterned fabric, cut the tails in a matching mix of color and pattern. With plain fabrics and

linings, lay the templates to make maximum use of the fabric.

3 Place the layers of fabric together in the same way as for swags but this time, machine stitch down three sides, leaving the top open.

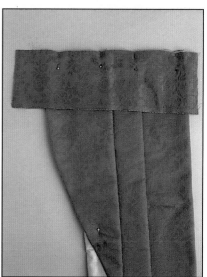

5 Pleat up and pin into place. Sew a 4 in (10 cm) wide strip of fabric to the top of the tail.

6 Attach the tails to the board with tacks or staples.

fabric 54 in (137 cm) wide

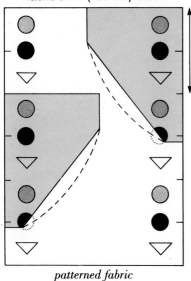

pattern repeat 25 in (64 cm)

fabric 54 in (137 cm) wide

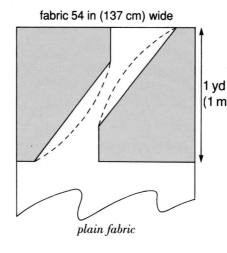

1 yd (1 m)

patterned fabric

plain fabric

Small tails to sit between swags can be made up in the same way as the end tails but using the following formula: 5 × the finished width, by the desired length. This will give two overlapping pleats on each side.

The tail tapers up from the middle, each side being half the depth of the center of the tail.

DRESS CURTAINS

Dress curtains are fixed curtains. They are not meant to be drawn across the window and are normally used in conjunction with a shade, blind, or sheer curtain that covers the window. Some are made to fit the window and are pulled together at the top and fixed back halfway down. These may have elaborate tiebacks and should be so precisely draped that to pull them would ruin their effect. Others are simply "mock" curtains fixed to the sides of the window. Make them look as though they could cover the window; one width on each side of a large window looks a little skimpy, even if there are sheer curtains in place, or a shade or blind to pull down at night.

Dress curtains are often used on bay windows with Roman or roller shades (blinds) covering the glass, where space is limited, and too much fabric would keep out the light. They are essential on a window with an arched top, although when the tiebacks are released the glass area would be covered.

Dress curtains are the solution if you have some beautiful patterned fabric, but not enough to cover the window two to three times. You can use the fabric to its best effect without overpowering the decorative scheme.

DOOR CURTAINS

*D*oor curtains are hung on the back of a door to keep out drafts and to muffle sound. These curtains are made up in the usual way and should be made in a very heavy fabric or interlined, and have an extra 4 in (10 cm) on the length. They are hung from portière rods, which are made to rise as the door is opened, so lifting the excess fabric from the floor and allowing the door to open.

Glass-fronted cupboard doors and internal clear glass doors sometimes have curtains fitted to them, acting both as a screen and a decoration. These are made with simple cased headings (see page 56) at the top and bottom. They are fixed on thin rods (wires), and kept taut lengthwise. If the curtain is to be seen from both sides, choose the fabric carefully; it must look good from the back as well as the front.

CAFÉ CURTAINS

*C*afé curtains are half-curtains that usually hang from a rod fixed across the window recess. They are mainly used in rooms that need privacy. They can also be used to hide an ugly view, and by covering the foreground they help focus the eye on distant hills or fields.

As café curtains are nearly always pulled across the window with the back showing through the glass, they should either be made from a fabric that looks good on both sides, such as gingham, sheers, weaves, or self-lined, or at least be given an attractive lining. They are made with simple cased headings with a pole through the gathered fabric, or scalloped headings, and pleated scallops which give a fuller gather, and are hung from rings and ties. Café curtains in kitchens close to cooking areas should have very little fullness.

MAKING SIMPLE CAFÉ CURTAINS

Materials
main fabric
contrast lining if necessary
rod to fit the window recess*

* There are special expanding rods made for café and shower curtains which are spring-loaded, so that the ends are held under tension against the recess. No other fittings are necessary and removal for cleaning is simple.

1 To calculate the fabric requirements, decide how full you want the curtains to be; one and a half times the length of the rod or pole is usually sufficient plus 1 in (2.5 cm) seam allowances. To calculate the length, measure from the top of the pole or rod to the sill plus 2 in (5 cm) for the cased heading, and ½ in (12 mm) for the seam allowance. Cut two pieces of fabric to these measurements.

2 With right sides together, machine the two pieces of fabric together around all sides, leaving a 6 in (15 cm) opening at the top of both side seams.

3 Turn right sides out through the gap and press well.

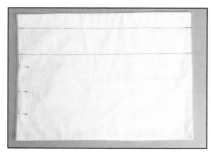

4 Machine stitch a line across the curtain, 2 in (5 cm) from the top edge. Now measure the pole and make another row of stitches the diameter of the pole or at least 3 in (8 cm) below the first line of stitches.

Alternatively, if you are unsure, measure from the sill to the pole base to determine the position of the casing. These two rows are the casing for the pole. A ruffle will form above the casing when it is gathered up on the pole.

5 Hand sew any raw edges, but do not sew across the casing.

6 Slide the curtain onto the pole or rod and hang.

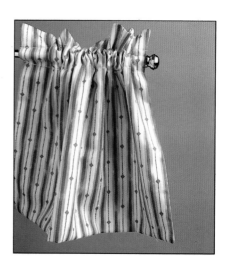

SPECIAL HEADINGS FOR CAFÉ CURTAINS

Materials

main fabric and lining
card for template
soft pencil
tape·measure
pole or rod
rings, ties, or loops*

* Ties and loops can be attached by machine to the gathered heading and then tied onto rings that are on the pole. They look good made up in a contrasting fabric which is also used to bind the hem of the curtain.

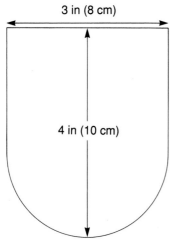

3 in (8 cm)

4 in (10 cm)

1 For a scalloped heading, make a card template for the scallop. A good size is 3 in (8 cm) wide and 4 in (10 cm) deep.

2 With right sides together, sew the two pieces of fabric together along the bottom edge. Draw a row of scallops ½ in (12 mm) from the top raw edge of the folded fabric with even spaces approximately 1½ in (4 cm) apart. For a pleated scallop, add 3 in (8 cm) to each space.

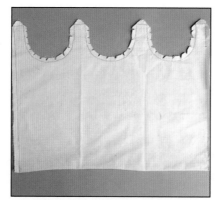

3 Machine stitch along the lines of the scallops and trim the seams, ¼ in (6 mm) from the stitching, notching the curves, and clipping any corners.

4 Machine stitch down one side and turn the curtain right side out. Press well and hand sew the other side opening.

5 For pleated scallops, make a pleat in the middle of each space between the scallop and secure with slip stitches.

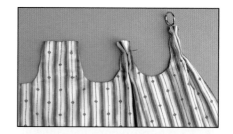

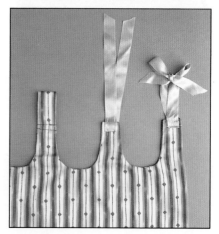

6 Sew the ring or fabric tie to the back of each scallop or pleat and either thread or tie onto the rod or pole to hang the curtain.

7 If you want to make a casing to thread the scallops onto a rod as for cased café curtains, then make the scallops twice as deep, say 8 in (20 cm) deep. When the curtain is made up, turn back the strips 3 in (8 cm) and machine stitch a loop for the rod to be threaded through.

SHEER CURTAINS

*T*hese are curtains made from sheer fabrics: they hang against the glass and are supplementary to the drawn curtains. Their purpose is to hide an undesirable view, give privacy, keep out strong sunlight or be purely decorative.

These curtains can be made from net, lace, or voile, in either cotton or synthetic fibers. They come in plain or patterned weaves, and are usually white or cream. Synthetic fabrics are lightweight, so do not economize on fullness.

Cotton fabrics will stay white, but may shrink when washed. Synthetic fabrics will yellow with age, but they wash well and stand up to strong sunlight.

These curtains may be made up as unlined,

machine-sewn curtains, with a synthetic tape or a fine curtain tape that suits the fine fabric. They will hang from conventional rods or tracks. Alternatively, they may be made to hang inside the window recess from expanding rods (wires).

The calculations given here make a 1 in (2.5 cm) casing with a heading where a ruffle (frill) is made above the casing. If you are making the curtain for a room where the heading is a feature, for example, in a bathroom or on a café-style curtain, make a higher heading. Only crisp sheers will stand up in this case. Lace will probably flop forward. However, this can be made a deliberate part of the curtain treatment. If the lace has a decorative edging, then allow at least 5 in (13 cm) for the heading and you will get a fake valance when the lace flops forward over the top of the curtain.

1 Measure the width of the window. Allow at least three times the window width for voiles and fine sheer fabrics; twice the width for medium weights and one-and-a-half for heavy cottons. If you are using lace panels, then add on only the hem and seam allowances, and plan carefully where the motifs are to be, so that you get the best effect when the panel is seen from the outside.

2 Measure the window length (drop) and add on 4½ in (12 cm) for hems and heading.

3 Fine netting, which comes in broad widths, can be made up sideways, using the length of the fabric rather than the width. This should avoid any seams. Cut out the fabric required, following the thread.

4 Fold over a double ½ in (12 mm) seam down either side and pin. Machine stitch through all thicknesses.

5 Fold up 1 in (2.5 cm) at the base and pin. Fold up a further 1 in (2.5 cm), pin and machine stitch.

6 Along the top edge, turn under ½ in (12 mm), then turn down 2 in (5 cm), and machine stitch along the hem line.

7 Machine stitch an additional row of stitches 1 in (2.5 cm) above this row of stitching to make the casing. This leaves a heading of 1 in (2.5 cm) above the casing.

8 Thread the rod (wire) through the casing and hang from hooks on either side of the window.

Materials

sheer fabric
fine machine needle and tissue paper*
matching thread
curtain rod (wire) the width of the window
two hooks attached to the window recess

* It is wise to sew sheer fabrics using a new machine needle of the finest size. This prevents pulled threads which can spoil the whole effect. Very fine fabrics are sometimes easier to sew if you place tissue paper between the fabric and the sewing machine plate.

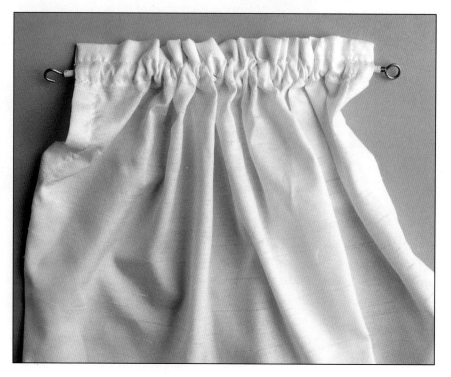

BRISE-BISE

This term, which means "blowing in the wind", is used for short net curtains that are bought with the top and base hem completed. Only the sides need to be hemmed.

STORE CURTAIN

This is a heavily patterned panel, usually made from cotton lace, often with a picture stitched into the lace, that hangs flat to the window without any fullness.

SHADES
(BLINDS)

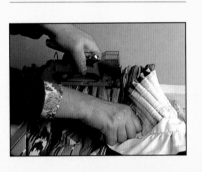

WINDOW SHADES (BLINDS)

*S*hades (blinds) come in many forms and with different names, such as Austrian, festoon, balloon, pull-up, Roman, and roller. The gathered shades (blinds), those that create flounces as they are drawn up, are ideal for romantic settings and elaborate window dressings. Roman and roller shades (blinds) give clean classical lines to any interior.

A festoon shade (blind) has fabric gathered horizontally and shirred vertically. It is often made from nets and laces. An Austrian shade (blind) is similar to a festoon, but uses less fabric (it has no vertical shirring), and is usually made from a lightweight cotton, silk, or polyester fabric.

Pull-up or balloon shades (blinds) have fabric gathered horizontally, but no vertical shirring. The effect is created by deep inverted pleats, which cause the shade (blind) to puff out along its base when it is pulled up. Many ruched shades (blinds) referred to as "Austrians" are in fact a mixture of these styles and designs.

— DETERMINING THE STYLE —

The original Austrian shades (blinds) were designed for tall windows and were made in fine laces or voiles, hung behind heavy curtains. Having increased in popularity in recent years,

60

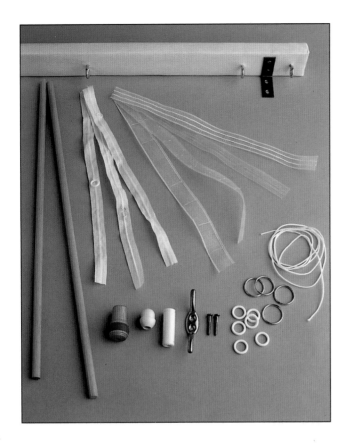

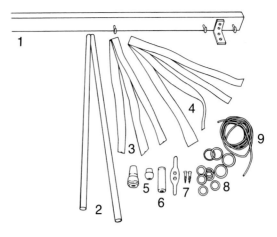

1 heading board
2 wooden poles for Roman blinds
3 festoon line tapes
4 tapes for sheer shades (blinds)
5 shade pulls
6 cord tidy
7 brass cleat and screws
8 brass and plastic rings
9 nylon cord

they are now made for windows of every shape and size and in every fabric. The really fussy ones are better for bedrooms; those with a more tailored look are suited to living areas.

When deciding on the style and design of an Austrian shade (blind) to suit a window, there are several questions to ask yourself. Do you want the shade (blind) to hang outside the window recess, inside the window recess, or inside the recess and with curtains? If you choose to have your shade (blind) inside the window recess, it will take light from the room by covering at least one third of the glass, whereas a shade (blind) fitted outside the recess may be fixed at various heights above the window, allowing more daylight into the room when raised (see page 62).

If you are choosing shades (blinds) to be used with curtains, the fabric for the shade (blind) should be lightweight and fairly plain.

Decisions need to be made about the heading tape too. The shade (blind) can hang from a cased heading threaded onto a pole (see page 65), or from a heading tape as for curtains when the shade (blind) is attached to a mounting board.

For some styles of window, such as a bay, a pole may be difficult to fit so a board would be more suitable together with a pencil-pleated heading tape. If you have curtains in the same room, match the heading of the shade (blind) to that of the curtains.

You need to ask yourself how you want the shade (blind) to look when it is fully lowered. It can be gathered vertically as a curtain; with a ruffle (frill) on the hem; with a scalloped edge; or with a ruched effect on the lower part of the shade (blind), as shown overleaf.

When deciding on the style of a festoon with its vertical gathers and horizontal ruches, you need to consider the degree of fussiness the room can take. A festoon can be made up in a sheer or lightweight fabric, permanently covering the window; very full with a heavy ruched effect; or not so full and using less fabric.

Remember that any ruched shade (blind) when raised will only be reduced by two thirds, therefore the more fabric you use in the length of the blind, the more glass will be covered when the shade (blind) is raised.

same hanging length (drop), different amounts of fabric

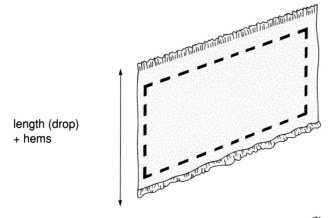

length (drop)
+ hems

**PLAIN GATHERED SHADE (BLIND)
WITH RUFFLE (FRILL) AT BOTTOM**

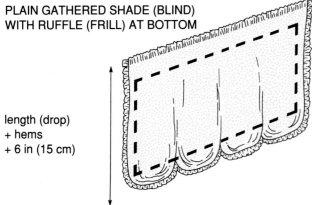

length (drop)
+ hems
+ 6 in (15 cm)

**BALLOON SHADE (BLIND) WITH RUFFLE
(FRILL) AT SIDES AND BOTTOM**

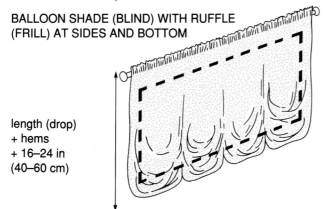

length (drop)
+ hems
+ 16–24 in
(40–60 cm)

AUSTRIAN SHADE (BLIND), NO FRILLS

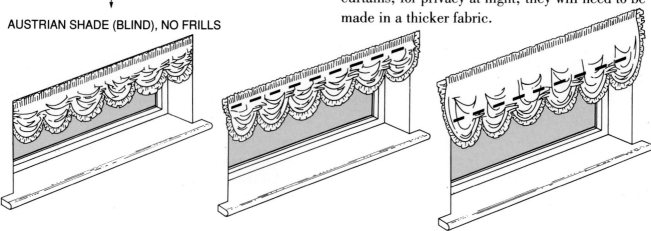

*fixing shade (blind) at different heights and with different
lengths of fabric*

You need to decide how full you want your shade (blind). It can be twice the window width using a thin fabric for a full swag or balloon; twice the window width with a thicker fabric for a very full swag or balloon; one-and-a-half times the window width with a thick fabric and full swag; or one-and-a-half times the window width for a thin fabric and slight swag.

Gathered shades (blinds) can be finished off with different decorations and accessories. Do you want ruffles (frills) on your shades (blinds) just along the hem; down the sides and along the hem; or in a contrasting color?

Having a ruffle (frill) down the sides of the shade (blind) will cover up the side cords and prevent a V shape developing. Ruffles (frills), however, do use a lot of fabric.

Other decorations include piping between the shade (blind) and the ruffle; binding on the ruffle; and bows or rosettes.

To fit a piped edge and a ruffle to a window shade (blind) can be time-consuming and quite difficult. Some sewing machines may not be able to cope with the thickness of fabric.

If the shades (blinds) are to be used with curtains, these will be better unlined and made of a fine fabric, as they must allow daylight through. Remember that these shades (blinds) will be seen from the outside with the reverse side of the fabric showing against the glass. How will your fabric look? Is it too patterned?

If the shades (blinds) are to be used with dress curtains, for privacy at night, they will need to be made in a thicker fabric.

Note: When raised the length (drop) is reduced by ⅔ only

CALCULATING THE SCALLOPS

Scallops are formed by rows of tape or rings sewn down the shade (blind), so the more scallops you want, the more rows of rings you will need. Where you sew the rows and how many rows of rings there are will determine the design of the scallop arrangement. Scallops should not be more than 12 in (30 cm) apart across the window (12 in/30 cm of gathered fabric). The larger the window, the larger the scallop size should be.

When choosing a design there are various possibilities. You can alter the size of the scallops to fit in with the window frame. For example, you can sew the middle two rows of rings closer together. Some scallops do not need a row of rings at the sides. This allows one side of the scallop to hang free. If you hang the shade (blind) outside the window recess, the free-hanging scallop will frame the window. By making the outer cords longer, the outer scallops will drop more. If the vertical rows of tape or rings are sewn close together across the shade (blind), it will be more ruched.

An alternative technique is to make up your shade (blind), gather it to fit the width of the window, and then, with the shade (blind) flat on a table, play with the scallops. See what looks best. Will three scallops look better than five? Does the fabric hang nicely without the side cords? Does it fall inwards? When you have the best effect, mark the rows for the rings or tape.

HANGING SYSTEMS

AUSTRIAN AND FESTOON SHADES (BLINDS) WITH TAPED HEADINGS

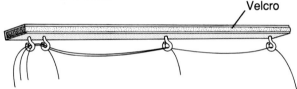

Velcro

covered board with screw eyes for cords and Velcro for fixing shades (blinds)

ceiling or recess fitting

wall fitting

ROMAN AND BALLOON SHADES (BLINDS)

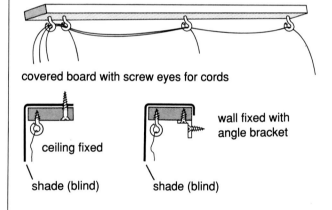

covered board with screw eyes for cords

ceiling fixed

wall fixed with angle bracket

shade (blind)

shade (blind)

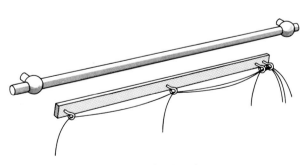

pole with batten fixed on wall below for screw eyes

AUSTRIAN AND FESTOON SHADES (BLINDS) WITH CASED HEADINGS

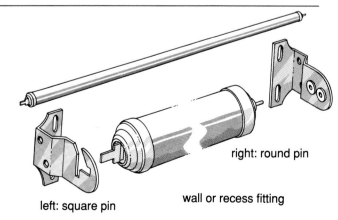

right: round pin

wall or recess fitting

left: square pin

ROLLER SHADES (BLINDS)

AUSTRIAN SHADE (BLIND) WITH RUFFLE

1 To calculate the fabric requirements, decide whether the shade (blind) is to be inside or outside the window recess. Measure the length plus 3 in (8 cm) for hems on a heading tape of 6 in (15 cm) for a cased heading. If you want an obviously scalloped edge, allow a further 6 in (15 cm), or for an extravagant ruched edge allow a further 15–24 in (40–60 cm). For the width, allow one-and-a-half to two-and-a-half times the window width depending on the thickness of the fabric and the effect you want.

2 Cut out the same amount of lining fabric.

3 Cut out a strip of main fabric for the ruffle (frill), 6 in (15 cm) by the width of the shade (blind) doubled for the hem, and four times the length for the sides.

4 Join any fabric widths where necessary. Avoid a center seam by placing half widths at each side.

5 Place the top fabric and lining together with right sides facing. Trim to exactly the same size.

6 Make up the ruffle (frill) (see page 14). Hide any joins by folding a gather over the join wherever possible.

7 If using piping (see page 38), sew it to the ruffle (frill). Do not sew too near the cord, and leave space for the final line of stitches.

8 Place the top fabric flat on the table, right side up. Pin the ruffle (frill) to the base, keeping all the raw edges together. You can take it up both sides too, in which case give each corner extra gathers and pin these securely. Take the ruffle (frill) right to the top of the shade (blind), and position the edges in this and the piping as unobtrusively as possible. Machine stitch together with a ½ in (12 mm) seam allowance. If piping is involved, use the appropriate foot on the machine.

9 With right sides together, lay the lining over the top fabric. Pull the lining well over the ruffle (frill) and pin the lining and top fabric together around all three sides. Machine stitch together from the top fabric side, just inside the row of stitches attaching the ruffle (frill) to the top fabric. Make sure the ruffle (frill) is well clear. Use a zipper foot if necessary.

10 Turn the shade (blind) right side out and press well.

11 To attach a taped heading, turn over the top hem allowance, and sew the tape along the top edge (see page 31) including the ruffles (frills).

12 For a cased heading, turn over the top hem allowance and sew the casing (see page 56). Make sure that the casing is large enough for the fabric to gather up on the pole.

13 If you have not yet decided on the scallop design, now is the time to "play" with it to get the effect you want. Lay the shade (blind) out flat, smooth it out and pin the two layers (lining and top fabric) together, pinning all over the shade (blind). Mark out the ring positions, keeping within the guidelines shown in the diagram below.

marking out the ring position

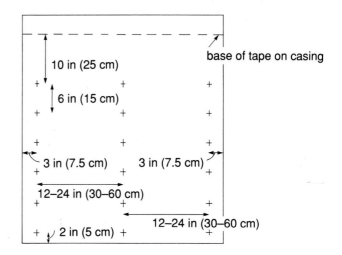

base of tape on casing

10 in (25 cm)

6 in (15 cm)

3 in (7.5 cm)   3 in (7.5 cm)

12–24 in (30–60 cm)

12–24 in (30–60 cm)

2 in (5 cm)

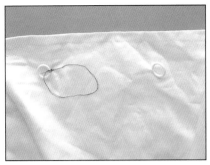

14 Hand sew the rings in the places marked, and using a waxed thread, sew through both layers of fabric, checking the front of the shade (blind) for neat stitches.

15 If using heading tape, fix a mounting board with angle brackets to the ceiling or recess or to the wall above the window. Gather up the tape to fit the board and insert screw eyes at intervals into the undersides of the board so they align with the tapes on the shade (blind). Allow for any returns.

16 Decide whether the shade (blind) is to pull from left or right. The cord running through the screw eyes furthest from the cleat will need to be longer as it has to go the length of the board.

17 Measure up and cut lengths of cord for each row of rings. Tie a cord to the bottom ring, thread it up through the rings and along the top, and pull from either the left or the right.

18 Hang the shade (blind) with strips of Velcro (see page 41) or staples to the board, making sure the eyelets are directly above the rings. Thread the cords through the screw eyes on the batten.

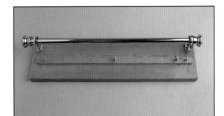

19 If the shade (blind) is being hung from a pole, the pole should be fixed inside the recess or mounted on the wall if the shade (blind) is hanging outside the recess.

20 Insert screw eyelets into the window frame or batten fixed behind and slightly below the pole.

21 When the shade (blind) is hanging, adjust the cords to get the scalloped effect you want, and tidy the ends, pleat the hanging cord ends, and thread through the acorn.

22 Fix a cleat to the wall to hold the cord tight and to keep the shade (blind) raised.

23 If the hem is to be kept scalloped, either tie the last two rings of each row together or, when the shade (blind) is hanging down as you want it, tie a large knot in the cords at the pulling side of the last screw eye. This will prevent the cords running through and will keep the hem scalloped.

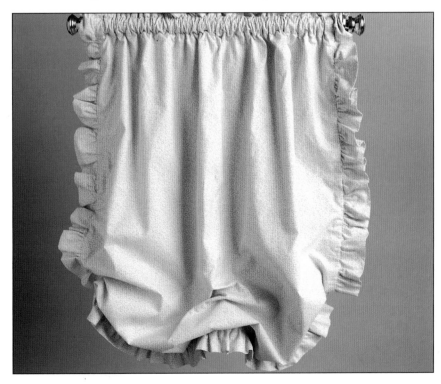

RUFFLED FESTOON SHADE (BLIND)

1 To calculate the fabric requirements, first decide whether the shade (blind) is to be inside or outside the window recess. Measure the drop and double it for sheer and fine fabrics, one-and-a-half times for not such a full look, plus 3 in (8 cm) for hems on a heading tape, or 6 in (15 cm) for a cased heading. For the width, allow twice to two-and-a-half times the window width.

2 Proceed as for Austrian shades (blinds) until step 13 but instead of sewing rings onto the curtain, lay the tape down the shade (blind) leveling up the rings or eyelets on the tape with the marked ring positions on the shade (blind). Pin the tape in place, keeping the fabrics smooth.

Turn the tape under at both ends, securing the internal cord well at the base, but allowing it to run freely at the top.

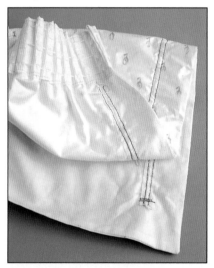

3 Sew the tapes in place with a row of stitches either side of the center cord, being careful not to sew over the cord.

4 When all the tapes are in place, pull the center cords in the tape, allowing the shade (blind) to gather up horizontally until it measures the length of the window. Fasten the cords off and roll them up neatly.

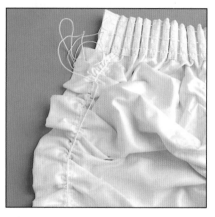

5 Proceed as for Austrian shades (blinds).

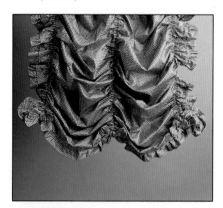

The two pictures above show the front and back of a small festoon (shade) blind. It has a piped and lined ruffle (frill) along the sides and bottom with piped bows at the base of each row of tapes.

PULL-UP SHADE (BLIND)

*P*ull-up or balloon shades (blinds) are really a pleated version of the Austrian shade (blind); where the Austrian has gathers, these have pleats.

When made in a fairly lightweight fabric, they will balloon out as the pleats unfurl at the base. They are much less fussy and can be interlined.

one fabric

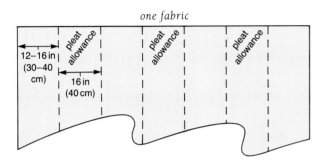

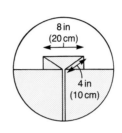

Materials

Same as for Austrian shades

1 To give these shades (blinds) the balloon effect, allow extra fabric in the width. The ideal pleat size is 8 in (20 cm) and these inverted box pleats should be placed evenly across the width of the shade (blind), 12–16 in (30–40 cm) apart. The number of pleats is determined by the size of the window and the style of window frame. To find the length of fabric required, measure the drop and add 5 in (13 cm) to cover the board and for the hems. Add a further 6 in (15 cm) for a slight scallop at the hem.

2 Measure the width of the window and for every pleat of 8 in (20 cm), add 16 in (40 cm) plus 1 in (2.5 cm) for seams. If a contrasting fabric is to be used for the pleats, cut these pieces 15 in (40 cm) wide, and give the main fabric extra seam allowances.

6 Turn the shade (blind) to the right side, and press well.

7 Pleat the shade (blind) up as designed, and press in place. Then pin and sew the pleats along the top edge of the shade (blind).

8 Baste (tack) the pleats together about 4 in (10 cm) below this.

9 Lay the pleated shade (blind) out with the lining facing up, and mark the rows of rings in the center of each pleat and 3 in (8 cm) from each side. Make sure that the rings all align horizontally. Hand sew all the rings in place, through all layers of fabric, using a waxed thread.

10 Cord the shade (blind) as shown on page 66.

11 Fix the mounting board and secure the shade (blind) on the top, so that it hangs over the edge and is kept clear of the glass. Remove the basting (tacking) from the pleats.

two fabrics

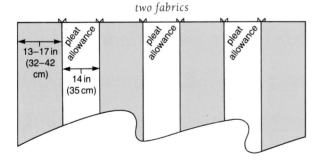

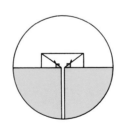

3 If two fabrics are used, cut them out and join them together with ½ in (12 mm) seams. Each strip of contrasting fabric should then be 14 in (35 cm) wide. The main fabric should just turn the corners of each pleat.

4 Cut out the lining and interlining (if they are to be used) to exactly the same measurements as the finished top fabric piece, i.e. after joining any contrasting fabric strips.

5 Lay the fabrics right sides together, the interlining with the top fabric. Pin them together, keeping the fabrics smooth, and machine stitch down both sides and along the hem.

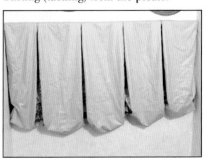

ROMAN BLINDS

*R*oman blinds are the most classical style. They fit into the smallest window space, cover very little glass even when hung in the window recess, and are extremely economical with fabric. They are particularly effective when used in bay windows, bays with low ceilings, and those with little or no wall space at the sides, as well as on windows where any other form of dressing would take away too much light. They may be used alone, alongside other Roman blinds or with dress curtains.

Roman blinds fold up and hang in pleats at the top of the window. Battens of wooden doweling, graphite, or plastic rods are stitched into pockets across the blind to keep these pleats straight and firm. The blind is fixed to the ceiling, window recess, or wall by a square wooden batten that holds the screw eyes for the cording system.

It is probably unwise to make these blinds any wider than 5 feet (1.5 meters); on larger windows more than one blind will be necessary. Remember to set the battens to run at the same level on all the blinds so they will all pleat up identically. Split the blinds to follow the window frame, making them either to the full width available, as close as possible together, or to fit over the glass, leaving the window frame showing.

Dress curtains set at each side of a bay window with Roman blinds can give an elegant look. However, make the dress curtains look as though they might just cover the window; don't let them appear skimpy.

Dress curtains or simple "bell pulls" (see page 71) may be hung between the blinds to add something to what would otherwise be a bare window during the day.

To decorate a Roman blind, you can either bind the edges all the way around in a contrasting color, or decorate the hem. A fringe, or a pleat made from either the same fabric as the blind or a contrasting one, are the most suitable. These edgings should be sewn on after the blind is made up. If they are fixed to hang below the hem of the blind, they will then show below the last pleat when the blind is pulled up and this must be taken into account when measuring for the length (drop). For example, if a fringe is to be attached to the hem of the blind and is to hang 2 in (5 cm) below the hem, 2 in (5 cm) must be taken off the length (drop) measurement; the finished blind will then drop exactly to the sill. Stitch the edgings on firmly as the pleating up and down of the blind will rub on this edging and crease it if it is not sewn on well.

A contrasting band could also be inset just inside the side and base edges of the blind.

Another decorative finish to a Roman blind is to sew the pockets on the front in a contrasting color. For example, an oriental-style scheme might have an off-white blind with pockets in dark gray or black across the front.

FABRICS

Roman blinds work well in most fabrics, from a really heavy canvas to a fine silk. The most important factor is for the fabric to be of a tight weave. Glazed chintz works well and also pleats well, but will have an almost quilted look when the blind is hanging down as the light deflects differently on the stitched lines across it. This can look quite attractive but not if you want a tailored smooth blind.

Roman blinds can be made in fabrics with all sorts of patterns, stripes being particularly suitable. It is most important for the pattern to be printed on the grain line. If the blind is to hang properly, it must be cut with the fabric on the straight of the grain; so if the pattern is slightly askew it will be very noticeable.

Plain fabrics can be used and these can be decorated with inserted borders, appliqué, and stencils. Muslin (calico) is the most versatile of fabrics as it works well and, once washed, will take the stencil paints readily.

The lining can be either any plain color or the traditional white or cream. Roman blinds can be interlined; this will make the blind much more bulky and heavy to pull up, and the pleats will not be nearly as sharp, but where extra insulation is important it might be necessary.

MAKING A ROMAN BLIND

Materials

main fabric	acorn
lining fabric	tacks or staples
any borders or decorative edging	soft pencil
wooden poles or battens,	metal or wooden yardstick
graphite or plastic rods	(meter ruler)
matching thread*	beeswax to strengthen thread
rings	
nylon cord, about twice the	* Make sure that you use threads
length of the row of rings	to match the fabric and that the
square wooden batten and	tension is correct on the
screws to secure it	machine. The stitching must be
screw eyelets	as unobtrusive as possible on
brass cleat	the front of the blind.

1 To calculate fabric requirements, measure the length (drop) of the blind and add 2–3 in (5–8 cm) for a turning at the top and a seam allowance. If the blind is dropping to the sill and is to have a pleat or decoration attached to the hem, allow for this in the length (drop measurement).

2 Measure the width of the window recess or the width that the blind is to cover, and add 1 in (2.5 cm) seam allowance.

3 Cut out the fabric and lining to the correct measurements, joining any extra fabric widths evenly on each side. The fabric must be cut on the straight grain, or the blind will not hang properly.

4 With right sides facing, pin, then sew the top fabric and lining together down both sides and along the hem. Trim and turn.

5 Press the blind well, making sure that no lining shows on the front edges.

6 Lay the blind on the table with lining face up, smooth the fabric out, and pin the two layers together all over.

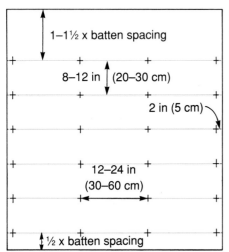

7 Mark the lining of the blind for the batten pockets by drawing a pencil line across the width of the blind. To give a pleat of 4–6 in (10–15 cm) in depth, batten pockets for the poles should be placed 8–12 in (20–30 cm) apart. They should be evenly

8 Make up the batten pockets from the lining fabric, cutting from the fabric lengthwise to make them stronger and less likely to wear. Cut them to the exact width of the blind and 4 in (10 cm) deep if you are using wooden poles as battens, or 3 in (8 cm) deep if using the narrower plastic or graphite rods.

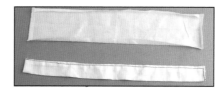

9 Fold in a ½ in (12 mm) seam all around the pocket fabric, fold it in half lengthwise, pin, then machine stitch on one side and along the full length of the pocket.

lines for batten placing and ring positions

spaced down the blind, leaving half a space at the hem and one-and-a-half spaces at the top, as shown in the diagram above, which also shows the spacing of the rings. On small blinds of two or three pleats, one space at the top is adequate.

10 Pin the fold of the pockets to the penciled positions on the back of the blind, keeping the fabric very smooth. The pockets should be ½ in (12 mm) from each edge of the blind. Baste (tack) along the pencil line first as a guide to the machine stitching. Machine stitch in place.

11 Cut lengths of wooden doweling or graphite or plastic rod to just short of the pocket length. Slide them into the pockets, and slipstitch the side opening.

12 Sew small plastic rings to the batten pockets across the blind at intervals of between 12 and 24 in (30 and 60 cm), depending on the width of the blind, and 2 in (5 cm) from each side. Wax the thread, and fasten the stitches off securely as these rings will take a lot of wear and tear.

13 Cord up the blind as shown on page 65.

14 Turn under the top raw edges of the blind, and staple to the top edge of the wooden batten. Lay the blind and batten face down, and insert the screw eyes into the base of the batten to align with the rings.

15 Fix the batten over the window by screwing through to the window surround, ceiling, or wall.

Inside the diagram (img_1):
1–1½ x batten spacing
8–12 in (20–30 cm)
2 in (5 cm)
12–24 in (30–60 cm)
½ x batten spacing

BELL PULLS

*T*hese are really no more than bows with extremely long tails. They can be made to fit any window and can add some decoration to what would otherwise be a plain window treatment. They can also hide an ugly window frame, and cover up untidy cords between shades (blinds). Bell pulls can be made in any fabric but look particularly good when made up in a border fabric. Several fabrics have borders and friezes manufactured in the same range, and these can be used for the bell pull.

In the photograph (right) bell pulls hang between a series of Roman blinds. This type of blind has been chosen to take maximum advantage of the light in a very sunny room. Bell pulls in a matching border fabric break up the area of glass.

Materials

main fabric
lining
interlining
wooden or brass curtain ring

---

1 Measure the length that the bell pull is to cover, double it, and add an allowance for the style of bow you want. The ideal width is about 6 in (15 cm).

2 Cut the fabric, lining, and interlining to these measurements, and allow 1 in (2.5 cm) on both the length and the width for a seam allowance.

3 Place the lining and top fabric right sides together with the interlining on top of the main fabric. Pin and machine stitch them together, leaving one of the short ends open.

4 Trim the corners, turn the bell pull to the right side, and press well.

5 Slipstitch the opening.

6 Pass one end of the bell pull through a large wooden or brass curtain ring and, with the ring in the middle, tie the bow over or around the ring and sew it firmly in place to keep the shape.

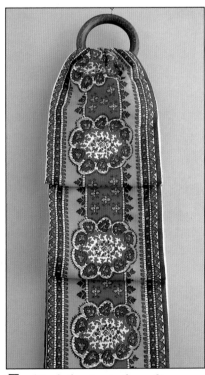

7 Attach the ring to the ceiling, wall, or window frame, wherever is appropriate.

ROLLER SHADE (BLIND)

*R*oller shades (blinds), with their clean straight lines, are the ultimate in functional window treatments. The spring mechanism enables them to cover or uncover the window instantly, filling the window space by night and disappearing to no more than a covered pole during the day. Kits to make these shades (blinds) are readily available, and comprise a roller containing the winding mechanism on the left side and a round pin on the right, two brackets, tacks, a batten for the hem, and a cord holder. The rollers come in several different lengths but may be cut down to the exact measurement of the window.

Roller shades (blinds) can be made from pre-treated fabrics, some of which are plastic coated so they are well suited to kitchens and bathrooms. They can also be made from any tightly woven furnishing fabric, as long as it is treated with some form of stiffening. These stiffenings can be either sprayed onto both sides of the fabric, or the fabric can be dipped into it. Obviously the pre-treated fabrics come in a limited range of colors

and patterns, but they do have the advantage of not fraying when they are cut.

Stiffened fabric will need side seams to prevent the edges from fraying. These will make the shade (blind) a little more bulky and its rise and fall a little less smooth if the fabric is too thick.

The majority of roller shades (blinds) are made in plain fabrics, but if you choose a patterned fabric, plan the layout of the pattern, centralizing any dominant markings and making sure that the hem has complete parts of the pattern. You could paint or stencil your own pattern onto a plain fabric, but wash the fabric first to remove all the finishes and always use fabric paints. Muslin (calico) is a versatile fabric, and with a subtle stencil on a pale cream background an individual shade (blind) can be created.

Roller shades (blinds) can have some form of decoration at their hems or the hem itself can be shaped. As with Roman blinds (see page 68), if the shade is to fall to the windowsill, the decoration on the hem must be taken into account when determining the drop measurement.

MAKING A ROLLER SHADE (BLIND)

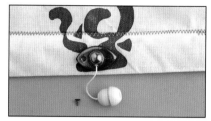

Materials

roller shade (blind) kit
chosen fabric
fabric stiffener, if necessary
metal tape measure*

* It is important to be very accurate when measuring and cutting the fabric.

5 Make a casing at the hem to hold the batten and zigzag-stitch it in place.

6 Stiffen the fabric if it is not pre-treated.

7 Tack or staple the fabric to the roller (follow the manufacturer's instructions).

8 Cut the hem batten just shorter than the width of the shade (blind) and slot it into place. Then stitch the ends closed.

9 Screw the cord holder onto the batten through the fabric and fit the cord and tassel.

10 Fix the brackets, either to the wall or to the window frame, with the bracket for the square pin on the left and that for the round pin on the right-hand side of the window.

11 Fit the roller into place with the fabric falling from the back, next to the glass.

12 Work the shade (blind) up and down several times, getting the tension correct, and altering the amount that is wound around the roller to obtain a perfect drop.

1 Calculate the size of the shade (blind) before you purchase the kit. If the shade (blind) is to be hung in the recess, measure across the recess width. If it is to be hung outside the recess, allow at least 1½ in (4 cm) on each side as this will give you space to attach the brackets and still cover the window recess. Buy the kit larger than these measurements and then cut it to the exact size.

2 To calculate the fabric requirements, measure the actual roller from end to end, and if you are not using pre-treated fabric, add 2 in (5 cm) to this measurement. Measure the drop to the windowsill, or 2 in (5 cm) below if the shade (blind) is to hang outside the recess. To this drop measurement, add 12 in (30 cm) for the roller to be covered when the shade (blind) is down and for a hem covering the base batten.

3 Cut out the fabric, making sure that the grain is running straight and that the piece of fabric is cut square. Use the corner of the cutting table or a T-square to check this. The shade (blind) will not hang well or function properly if these points are not observed.

4 If using untreated decorator fabric, fold a 1 in (2.5 cm) turn-in on each side. Then, using a zigzag stitch, machine stitch in place.

ALTERNATIVE EDGINGS

*T*here are numerous different shapes suitable for the bottom edges of roller shades (blinds). These edgings decorate the shade (blind) below the batten, but some have various cut-out shapes with a bottom bar keeping the base together.

The simplest treatment for the bottom edge is some sort of fringe which can be glued to the fabric covering the batten. Remember that if the shade (blind) drops to the sill without a straight base, light will show through.

When deciding on the shape of the bottom edge of your shade (blind), try to use the pattern of the fabric as a guide; follow the shape of a flower, of squares with a checked design, of rounded curves with a flowing pattern. Make the shapes correspond to the pattern.

TO MAKE A DECORATIVE WAVY EDGING

Materials

as for the roller shade (blind)
paper for template

1 Cut out the roller shade (blind) fabric to the length (drop measurement) less the depth of the shaped edging.

2 Turn in the side seams and zigzag-stitch as for the roller shade (blind).

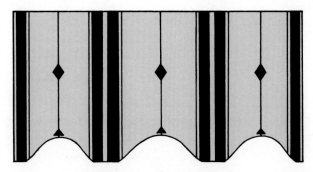

template

3 Cut out a paper template for the wavy edging as, for example, in the diagram above. It is easier to cut a template for half the edging and then cut the fabric on the fold to get a symmetrical shape. The best finished depth should be about 5 in (13 cm). Plan to have either the crest or the dip in the wave in the center of the shade (blind). Use the shape of a plate to get a good edge if your freehand curves are not good enough.

4 Cut two pieces of the shade (blind) fabric 1 in (2.5 cm) wider than the finished shade (blind) and 2 in (5 cm) longer than the template. If possible the pattern on these two pieces of fabric should be identical.

5 Fold one piece of fabric in half and, using the template, cut out the shaped edge with the template against the fold. Leave an allowance of ½ in (12 mm) all around.

6 Cut out the other piece of fabric using the first as a pattern.

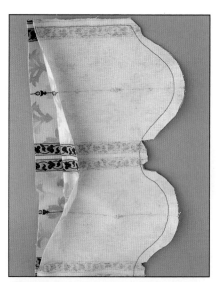

7 With right sides together, sew these two pieces together along the two sides, and at the shaped edge trim and notch the seams on the corners. Turn the fabric right side out and press well. This edging should now be exactly the same width as the shade (blind).

8 Cut a strip of fabric to cover the batten, approximately 3 in (8 cm) deep (this depends on the size of the batten) and the width of the shade (blind) plus 2 in (5 cm) for the side seams. Turn in the side seams and zigzag-stitch together.

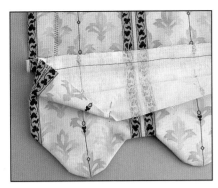

9 Sew this strip to the top of the back side of the prepared edging.

10 Sew the top of the other side of the edging to the bottom of the shade (blind).

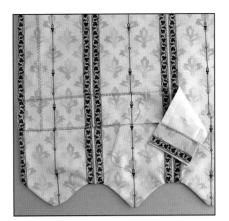

11 Press the attached strip upward and oversew the top to the back of the main shade (blind) fabric using a zigzag stitch across the edge.

12 Stiffen the fabric either by dipping or spraying.

13 Attach the stiffened fabric to the roller.

14 Slot in the batten, and attach the pull cord as for the roller shade (blind).

THE BATTEN BELOW THE EDGE

When the shaping is such that the batten is fixed below the decorative edging, make the shade (blind) and edging as follows:

1 Extend the drop measurement by approximately 4 in (10 cm).

2 If you are not using a pre-stiffened fabric, turn in and sew the side seams.

3 Cut the template for the edging to include 4 in (10 cm) for the batten casing.

4 Using the template, shape the bottom of the shade (blind), giving a seam allowance of ½ in (12 mm) all around.

5 Using the template, cut out one piece of fabric for the edging facing, also with a ½ in (12 mm) seam allowance.

6 Place the facing onto the bottom of the shade (blind), right sides together, and machine stitch around the edging with a ½ in (12 mm) seam.

7 Trim and notch where necessary and turn right side out.

8 Press well and sew the top of the facing to the main shade (blind) fabric using a zigzag stitch.

9 Fold the fabric back to form the casing for the batten, and machine stitch two rows of stitching to form the loops.

10 Finish the shade (blind) as before.

As an alternative edge treatment, try adding four strips of fabric, each separately attached to the main fabric and linked by an extra piece of dowel.

Shade pulls

Any number of decorative accessories can be attached to the cord for pulling the shade (blind) up and down, the most common being the crocheted ring and the wooden acorn. Be careful of ceramic acorns; being heavy, they do have a tendency to swing into the glass. Other ideas include tassels, macramé knots, large beads, even strings of small beads, or small wooden animals, which are fun to use in a child's room.

CHAIR COVERS

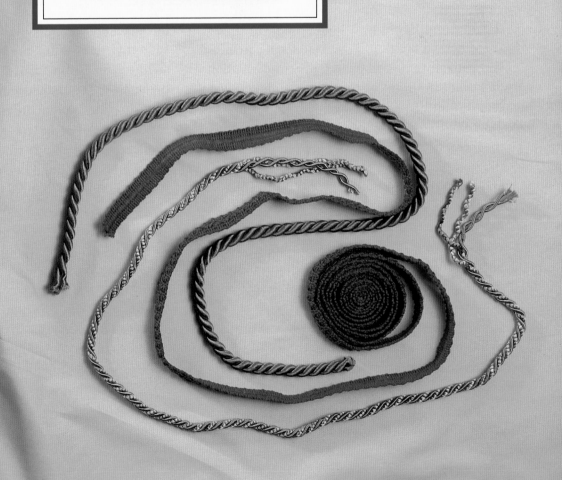

SLIPCOVERS (LOOSE COVERS)

Slipcovers (loose covers) need not be a daunting prospect if you take them carefully and patiently step-by-step. Plenty of imagination and common sense can transform the dullest and oldest chair into an attractive addition to any room. To be able to remove the covers makes them practical and versatile: different covers for the same chair make it adaptable for any room and create varying atmospheres. For example, light fabrics can be used for sunny summer days, formal fabrics and styles for reception rooms, or warm fabrics for winter months. Thus a dining chair, when not being used at a table, can be stored in any other room and harmonize perfectly in its new surroundings.

The style of cover for an armless dining or bedroom chair can be varied to suit the mood of the room. A straight skirt to the floor, kick-pleated at the corners, creates an elegant, formal image. Ruffled (frilled) skirts need not be relegated to the bedroom. By choosing colors carefully, you can bring a lighter note to a formal setting. This is especially useful when dining and living areas are in the one room. Box-pleated skirts are ideal for bedrooms.

Choosing the right type of fabric for cleaning and sewing purposes is important. A very thick, heavy fabric gives an extremely bulky seam – with piping and a lined skirt and pleats you could be faced with nine layers to stitch through. Therefore it is necessary to use a fabric that is pliable but hard wearing. However, too loose a weave will allow too much stretching. Highly finished fabrics, such as glazed cotton or heavily dressed canvas, lose their shine through wear and cleaning and are very hard on the sewing machine. Linen, linen blends (union), cotton (preferably pre-shrunk), damask, closely woven wool, fine corduroy, soft canvas, or light chintzes are the most suitable fabrics.

DROP-IN SEAT COVER

*I*f you have a wooden chair, you can make a tie-on cushion that just covers the seat (see page 81), or add a ruffle (frill) to come partway down the legs, or cover the legs completely by making the skirt to the floor. If your dining chairs have drop-in seats, the cover is tacked to the underside of the seat, leaving the rim of wood showing, or else, on an upholstered seat, the fabric is secured underneath the frame.

Most fabrics are suitable for a drop-in seat; avoid bulky fabrics as once they are folded over the sides the seat may be too tight for the frame. As drop-in seats are usually on dining chairs, and have a lot of use, choose fabric that can be easily sponged clean after being treated with spray stain protector.

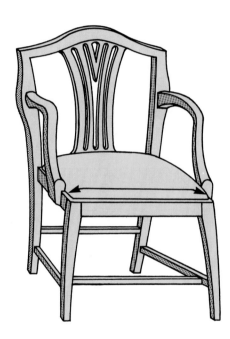

4 Make sure there are no wrinkles or baggy patches on the right side, and turn the seat over. Tack or staple the overlap of fabric around the edge into the wooden frame. The tacks or staples should be about 1½ in (4 cm) apart.

5 Complete the corners by opening out and tacking at the corner. Trim away the excess, then fold in the two edges to make a tidy fold across the corner.

Materials

decorator (furnishing) fabric
tacks and hammer or staple gun
muslin (calico) lining if desired

1 Remove the seat and check that the padding is in good condition. If there is any looseness, either take it to an upholsterer for re-upholstering or strip and insert a piece of good-quality foam rubber. (The foam will have to be covered with muslin (calico) before the top fabric can be tacked in place. The method is the same as for the seat cover.)

2 Measure the seat at its widest point from the bottom edge and add 3 in (8 cm) extra all around. Cut out a square to these measurements and lay it over the seat. Any pattern should be centered in the square before cutting out. The grain of the fabric should run from front to back.

3 With the fabric face up on the seat, fold over to the edge and lightly tap in a tack at the center of the back edge. Pulling the fabric taut from the top, repeat this for the other sides. This temporary tacking holds the fabric in place while you secure it permanently underneath.

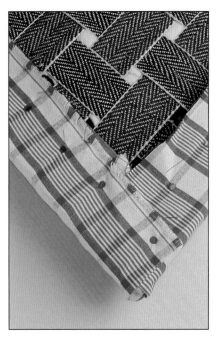

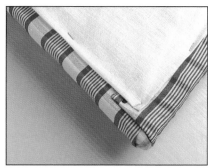

6 For neatness underneath, you can cut out a rectangle of lining fabric adding 1 in (2.5 cm) all around for the hem, and secure this with tacks or staples on top of the raw edges of the cover fabric.

7 Press the top if necessary, although the tautness of the fabric should prevent any creasing.

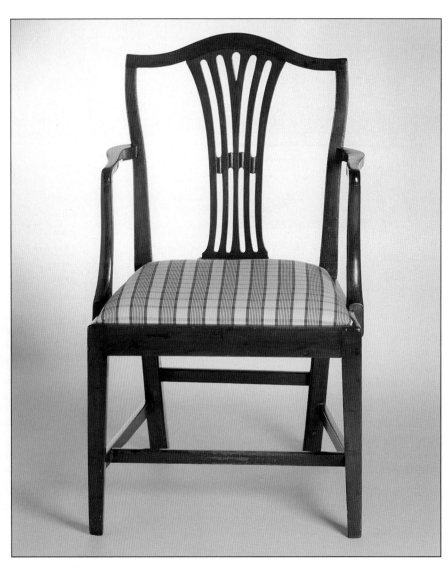

TIE-ON SEAT COVERS

This method of covering a dining chair is suitable for drop-in seats or upholstered chairs and it does not use any tacks or staples to secure the fabric – merely ties around the back legs – making it easy to remove and launder. As it is quick to do, you could make two sets of covers: one formal and one informal. Any fabric suitable for an armless chair cover will work.

Materials

decorator (furnishing) fabric
matching thread
pins

---

1 Check that the chair is not lumpy. If so, it will need re-upholstering. Measure the chair seat at its widest point from the bottom edge and add 3 in (8 cm) extra, or the depth of the seat plus seam allowance, all around. Cut out a square of fabric to these measurements. Remember to center any pattern.

2 Place the fabric right side up on the chair seat and smooth down the sides and front. Secure with pins.

3 Pin darts down the front corners to take up excess fabric. Take the pins right down to the base of the seat.

4 Anchor the fabric along the back with pins close to the uprights. Gently ease the fabric around the wood, clipping to within ⅛ in (3 mm) of the wood, sparingly, in order to assist the curving of the fabric. Mark the fold line around the wooden uprights of the chair with pins. Repeat on the other side.

5 Mark with a line of pins ⅛ in (3 mm) below the edge of the chair for the hem line.

6 Remove the pins and take off the cover. Reverse the front darts to the inside and machine stitch them.

7 Cut two strips of fabric on the bias, 12 in (30 cm) long and 1½ in (4 cm) wide, for finishing around the back uprights. With right sides together, pin the strip to the fabric along the line of pins. Machine stitch the facing and the cover together. Trim the raw edges of facing and cover. Clip the corners, turn the facing to the inside and press. Repeat for the other side. Fold in the raw edges and machine stitch.

8 Fold under the hem of the cover to the inside along the marked pin line and press. Turn in the raw edges and pin them.

9 To make the ties for the back, cut four strips of fabric 12 in (30 cm) long by 2½ in (6 cm) wide. With right sides together, stitch along one end and down the other side allowing ¼ in (6 mm) seam allowance. Clip seams and turn right sides out. Press.

10 Check the seat cover for fit and mark where the ties should go on either side of the back legs. Pin the four ties under the hem at the marked positions at the back legs.

11 Machine stitch the hem all around making sure the ties are firmly caught under the hem.

F I N I S H I N G   T O U C H E S

Bows could be used instead of ties. Either bows or ties can be placed at the front as well as at the back legs for an extra decorative effect. Allow extra contrast or matching fabric as necessary.

The four bows could be attached to the corners of the seat with Velcro to make it easier to match front to back in terms of size and shape. The cover still needs to be secured to the uprights. To do this, make a very small tie, just long enough for the ends to overlap at the back of the upright.

Stitch Velcro to both ends, so that it can be wrapped around the upright and fastened. Stitch more Velcro on top of these loops and at the two front corners. Make up the bows, stitch on Velcro and attach.

Braid, fringe, or other contrast edging can be stitched to the hem.

A ruffle (frill) may be added to the sides and front, in which case remember to allow extra for seam allowances.

POUFFE COVER

Fabrics that are suitable for chair covers or curtains are ideal for a pouffe or hassock cover. These look tailored if piping is inserted into the horizontal seams around the gusset. The same method can also be used to cover a stool, for example in a bedroom.

Materials

decorator (furnishing) fabric
matching thread
piping, see page 38

---

1 Measure each section as for a cushion with gusset (see page 19), but allow for only one top and the gusset (without zipper). Measure for a skirt as for the tailored skirt (valance) with inverted pleats at the corners (see page 96).

2 Allowing for pattern repeats, calculate the fabric requirements. Add extra fabric for self piping or use a contrasting fabric in the same weight.

3 Cut one piece for the pouffe top and four gusset sections. (There is no need for a zipper.) Allow ½ in (12 mm) for seam allowances.

4 Make a length of piping long enough to go around the top of the pouffe cover twice (if you are adding piping at top and bottom of gusset) or once (for piping bottom of gusset only). If piping the top, pin a length of piping all around the top section on the seam allowance, raw edges together. Join the piping (see page 13).

5 Lay the top section right side down on the pouffe. Pin the four gusset sections to the top and pin the corner seams so the cover fits accurately and tightly.

6 Ease the cover off. Machine stitch the gusset to the top using a zipper foot to enclose the piping and sew the corner seams. Trim the seams evenly and notch to ease the fit especially at the corners. Press.

7 With right sides out, replace on pouffe and check the top for fit and pin a line along the gusset where the skirt is to be fitted.

8 Using the remainder of the piping, pin, baste (tack) and machine stitch the piping along the marked line for the skirt, placing raw edges together.

9 Machine stitch the four skirt sections together to make a continuous circle of fabric. Put the cover back on the pouffe, wrong sides out, and starting from the center of each side pin the skirt to the top. At the corners, take up the excess fabric and make the inverted pleat, making sure the pleat aligns with the corner seam on the top. Pin everything securely with the pins along the line of piping.

10 Remove the cover and machine stitch the skirt to the top using the zipper foot. Trim the seams and press.

11 Put the cover back on the pouffe right side out and mark the hem line. Hem as for curtains (see page 31).

Any of the skirt variations suitable for a bed dust ruffle (valance) (see page 94) can be used on a pouffe cover. A round pouffe or stool cover is made in the same way. This looks good with box pleats all around (see page 96).

The seat of this wooden stool has been padded with a foam cushion and the circular gusset section is piped at top and bottom. A full-gathered skirt completes the effect.

MAKING A SLIPCOVER (LOOSE COVER)

The basic methods for making slipcovers (loose covers) can be applied to a four-seater sofa or a small armchair. You can also adapt the method to an armless chair. The thing to remember is to be methodical, do not skimp on fabric, and treat the furniture to be covered as you might a tailor's dummy – every piece is fitted on the furniture before moving on to the next. The main difference is the tuck-in section where the back of the chair meets the seat. There is usually a space here where the cover is tucked well down.

Do not be tempted to use cheap unsuitable fabric. All your efforts will be wasted. Linen blends (union) and similar good-quality upholstery fabrics are best for the job.

If there are slipcovers (loose covers) already on the piece of furniture, unpick the seams, and adding a generous seam allowance, use these as a pattern. If the piece is upholstered you will need to make a paper pattern.

The skirt can be lined to add body and to make it hang well. However, if you decide to box pleat all around, use a lightweight lining.

This method makes a cover for the whole piece of furniture and then the skirt is added on top. The base of the cover is held taut by a drawstring around the bottom edge, which secures the cover underneath the chair.

M a t e r i a l s

decorator (furnishing) fabric
matching thread
long zipper or Velcro strip*
paper for pattern, such as newspaper
piping in same weight of fabric
lining for the skirt section
length of strong cord for drawstring

* Measure the length of the outer left back seam from the top to the floor less 2 in (5 cm).

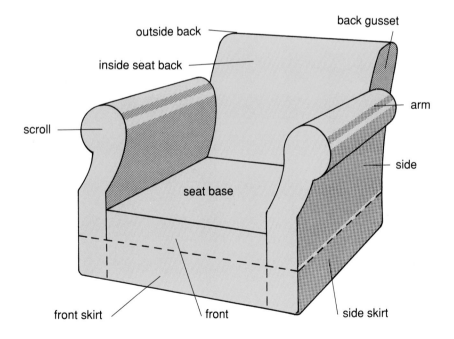

the parts of an armchair

1 Measure up and draw all the sections of the chair onto paper. Cut the paper pieces out, allowing 1 in (2.5 cm) all around for seams, and calculate the amount of fabric required. Use the existing cover to determine where the seams are to go. The pieces should include outside back, inside seat back, seat base, front, scrolls, arms, sides, and front and side skirts (this depends on the design). The outside back, front, and sides should be long enough to tuck under the chair and have a drawstring casing made. So add 6 in (15 cm) allowance at the bottom.

2 If adding a skirt cut the skirt sections out in the top and lining fabric. The skirt should be the finished length plus ½ in (12 mm) seam allowance at the top where it joins the cover, and 1¼ in (3 cm) at the hem line. Measure around all four sides of the base of the chair. Add an allowance for the required number of pleats. Remember that even if adding a straight skirt, there will be an inverted pleat at each corner. Add ½ in (12 mm) seam allowances, for each join to be made in the skirt lengths. On a square armed chair or sofa the arms will be divided into inside and outside pieces and an armrest section.

Chairs come in so many shapes and sizes that you will need to look carefully at yours before cutting out the fabric. To be really accurate, if you are a beginner, cut the pattern in muslin (calico) or other cheap lining fabric.

3 Pin each pattern piece to the chair and mark where the seams go. Use this pattern to cut out the main fabric, making sure any pattern is centered on the back or seat areas. Leave plenty of extra fabric at the seams on those parts of the cover that will tuck in – at least 8 in (20 cm). As each piece is cut, label it clearly for future reference.

4 Measure all the visible seams for the length of piping. Make up this amount of piping (as described on page 38).

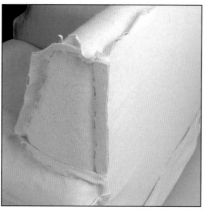

5 The cover is pinned with all fabric pieces right sides up and seams showing while you are getting a good fit. These are then reversed when sewn. Make sure the pattern is the right way up and aligned. Pin the inner and outer back sections to the chair and pin the seam along the back. You may need to gather the fabric or make darts for a good fit. (There may even be a welt along the back in more modern designs.) The outer back will be long at the sides; this is later joined up to the armrests and sides.

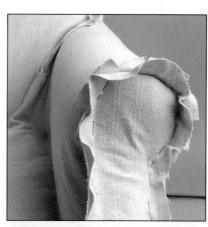

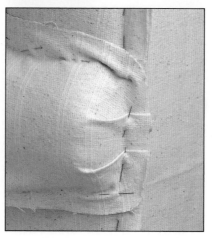

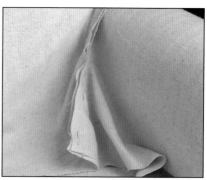

6 Continue to pin the seams together. The only seam that will not be tight against the chair is the tuck-in around the seat. Leave these long flaps. Trim the seams evenly to 1 in (2.5 cm) all around. Make notches in the raw edges at 3 in (8 cm) intervals. These serve as references when you turn the seams right sides together. Take the cover off.

7 Unpin the tuck-in seam, keeping the pins in position on one side. Reverse the seam and stitch, matching the notches and keeping the edges even.

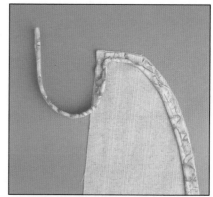

8 Now stitch the piped seams, allowing 1 in (2.5 cm) of piping cord at the beginning and end of each seam. To do this, baste (tack) the piping to the relevant pieces once you have unpinned them and before they are joined and stitched to the adjacent pieces. Remember to allow the full length of piping at the outer back seams.

9 Continue to unpin, insert piping, and machine stitch all the seams. Check the fit after every seam has been sewn and make any adjustments necessary.

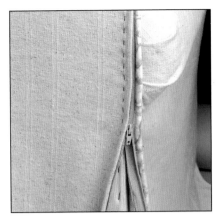

10 The back left seam is usually where the zipper is inserted. Sew down about 5 in (13 cm) from the top back. Set the loose end of piping to one side of the seam and turn back the other raw edge. The zipper should open from the bottom up. Insert as for piped cushions (see page 13). If you decide to use Velcro, sew the strips along the seam allowance, covering the raw edges.

11 Put the cover back on the chair and check that the surplus fabric around the bottom is the same amount all around. Mark with pins where the chair legs come. Remove the cover and clip away the fabric to fit around the legs leaving a ¼ in (6 mm) seam allowance. Finish these edges with a machine-stitched hem or a strip of bias-cut fabric (see page 122).

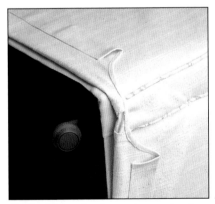

12 Make the drawstring casing by turning back ½ in (12 mm) along the raw edges and then a further 2 in (5 cm). Machine stitch each section to make a casing. Thread a cord through it. The cord will come out of one casing and back in again around the legs or feet of the chair or sofa.

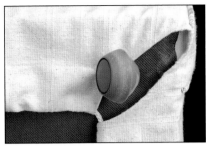

13 Put the cover back on again and tie the drawstring to secure. Push the tuck-in section well down between the seat and back. Check for any wrinkles and make sure the piping is lying straight.

14 If you are adding a skirt, mark a row of pins where it is to be attached. Pin, baste (tack) and sew a length of piping along the skirt seam line with the piping facing away from the hem.

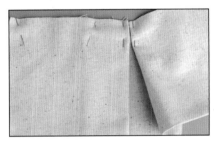

15 Join the skirt sections together, allowing the appropriate amount for corner inverted pleats or box pleats all around if preferred (see page 96). Join the lining sections too.

16 With right sides together, join the lining and skirt together along three sides allowing a ½ in (12 mm) seam allowance. Turn right sides out and press. Pin the two raw edges together.

17 Remove the cover and, starting at the center front, pin the skirt to the cover along the piped seam line. Work toward the corner inverted pleats.

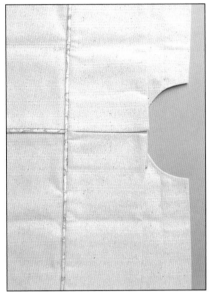

18 Machine stitch the skirt to the cover.

19 Finish all seam allowances and press.

BEDS

*B*EDSPREADS

*T*he most prominent piece of fabric in a
bedroom is often the bedspread, so it should
be carefully chosen when creating a new look.

The fabric used will depend on whether a
washable one is needed – are dogs, cats, or
children involved? From this it is easier to
determine what fabric to buy. The fabric should
complement the curtains; it can even be the same
fabric or a coordinating pattern. The most suitable
fabrics are medium-weight cottons in patterned
chintz or, if you want impact for a rather subdued
room, choose a bold geometric. Lightweight wool
in warm colors and patterns, such as paisley or
rich textured weaves, creates immediate warmth
and comfort while crisp cottons are cool, pretty,

and create the feeling of space. In pure white
cotton, bedspreads look very smart, especially
when a bright lining is used for interest and color.
Cotton can be made heavier and more substantial
by interlining, and even quilting, for which a
layer of fiberfill batting (wadding) will be added.
Interlining will prevent a dark lining from showing
through the top fabric.

A bedspread can look bulky if used over a
duvet, and a fitted one would not be suitable as
the bulk underneath distorts the line. If you think
that a thick bedspread is too untidy, a thickly
crocheted afghan (throwover) can look most
effective or, perhaps a lace cover with the
color of your duvet cover showing through.

A Plain Unlined Bedspread

*T*his is the simplest to make. A bedspread usually covers the whole bed, and touches the floor at the sides and foot. If, however, there is a dust ruffle (valance) fitted to cover the frame, finish the spread just below the top of that skirt (valance) (about 8 in/20 cm off the ground). The corners of the cover should be gently rounded to give a softer line, and the edges can be scalloped, finished with a fan edge or ruffle, or bound.

The measurements of all bedcovers are taken over a made-up bed. Because of the width of most decorator (furnishing) fabrics, it will probably be necessary to join widths. The seams are generally made at the sides of the top section.

Materials

main fabric
matching thread
bias strip to bind the edge if
desired

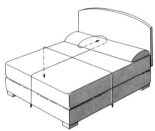

1 Measure the length and width of the bed, plus the drop to the floor, or the required length and width, remembering to add a tuck-in of about 18 in (46 cm) under the pillow. If a pillow flap is required (this means that the fabric cover goes under the pillow and over again, tucking in front) add a further 35 in (90 cm). An extra 2 in (5 cm) should be added for the hem all around.

2 Cut two widths of fabric to the required measurements. Cut one in half lengthwise, and with right sides together, join at the selvages on either side of the center panel.

3 If matching a pattern, cut out one width, and then match the pattern (see page 32) before cutting. Make sure the pattern is running in the same direction.

4 If the cover is to be unlined, press the seams to one side and topstitch to anchor the raw edges.

5 Press and turn up a ½ in (12 mm) hem, then a 1½ in (4 cm) hem. Miter the corners (see page 33) if necessary. Machine stitch all around the cover.

6 For rounded corners, put the cover over the bed, and pin a line where it touches the floor at the corners of the bed. Use a large dinner plate or some other round object about

12 in (30 cm) in diameter as a template to neaten the curve. Cut away the excess fabric leaving a hem allowance of 2 in (5 cm). Turn a double hem all around, and notch the corners to remove excess fullness. Machine or slipstitch to finish.

If the bed has a footboard, a bedcover will be rather bulky at the corners. To avoid this, simply make the bedspread as described, but join only half a width across the width of the bed, making the join so that it is hidden under the pillow. Remember this when calculating how much fabric to buy. Miter all the outside corners.

MAKING A LINED
AND INTERLINED BEDCOVER

*I*nterlining will make the cover heavier and more sumptuous as well as being more practical for winter nights. The lining can be made up in a contrasting color or even a co-ordinating small, patterned cloth to match the scheme in the room. When the bedcover is turned back, the reverse will be both practical and decorative. This bedcover will have to be dry cleaned. The method for making is rather like interlined curtains (see page 32).

Materials

main fabric
lining
interlining
matching thread
contrasting fabric for decorative
edging – ruffle (frill) or binding
tailor's chalk

1 Calculate the fabric requirements and make up as for the plain bedspread to step 4. Press the seams open. The hem allowance should be only ½ in (12 mm) all around.

2 Cut out the required widths of lining to the same measurements.

3 Cut out and join with zigzag or herringbone stitch the widths of interlining (see page 32).

4 Join interlining to top fabric with lockstitches (see page 33).

5 To finish off with binding, join the lining to the interlined top fabric with wrong sides together, and pin all along the hem line to keep the layers together.

6 Calculate how much binding is needed by measuring twice the length and twice the width of the cover. Cut out and join enough bias strips of contrasting fabric to make up the required finished width plus 1 in (2.5 cm) for seams.

7 Place the strip along the top of the cover, right sides together. Pin and machine stitch along the seam allowance. Trim away excess fabric from seam allowance, and press the seam away from the cover.

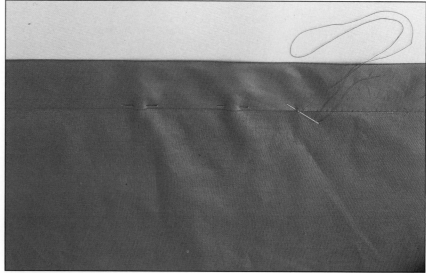

8 Turn the binding to the wrong side of the cover, turn in the raw edges for ½ in (12 mm), pin and press. Slipstitch to finish off the hem just above the seam, working the slipstitches into the machine stitching.

9 To finish off with a ruffle (frill), lockstitch in the interlining, but do not attach the lining. Find and mark the center point on each side and the foot end.

10 Calculate how much ruffle (frill) is needed by measuring twice the length and the width of the cover at the foot of the bed. Decide on depth of ruffle, and add 1 in (2.5 cm) for seams. Decide on whether it is to be single or double (see page 14).

11 Divide the ruffle (frill) into four equal sections. Stitch in four sections along one long edge with two rows of gathering stitches. Gather up to create fullness.

12 With right sides together and raw edges matching, pin the ruffle (frill) around the hem, along the sides and the foot end, using center points as a guide. Ensure the gathers are evenly distributed with slightly more gathers at the corners.

13 Machine stitch the ruffle to the bedcover allowing a ½ in (12 mm) seam allowance.

14 Lay the cover flat on a large surface, right side up and ruffle (frill) facing in toward the center. Cover with the lining, right side down, and pin all around the edges. The lining may appear not to fit at this stage because of the bulk of fabric.

15 Using the row of stitches as a guideline, machine stitch the lining to the cover, leaving an opening on one side.

16 Turn right sides out and press. Slipstitch the opening closed.

To apply a braid or fringe, pin it all around the edge, so that the frame of the edging aligns with the finished hem. Machine along the top of the edging with a matching thread.

DUST RUFFLES (VALANCES)

A gathered or tailored dust ruffle (valance) is designed to cover the frame and bed legs, and make the bed even more attractive. A flounced or box-pleated dust ruffle (valance) is easy to make, but choose the fabrics carefully. Large repeat patterns are lost when pleated; small compact or one-way designs are more suitable. Plain and patterned cotton and glazed chintzes are widely used for box-pleated and inverted pleats, while unlined pastel lace, voile, and other sheer fabrics, when generously gathered, give a softer appearance. Velvets, tweeds, and wools can be used if a divan is to be utilized as a daybed in a study, possibly with a bolster (see page 17).

Beds like these are often used as sofas for day use, therefore a hard-wearing skirt (valance) would be more suitable to withstand soiling and wear. Gathered dust ruffles (valances) are more informal, and those with an inverted pleat at the two end corners give a tailored finish. These can all be finished with a braid, border, or fan edge, or contrast-bound for extra impact. A contrast piping line at the seam allowance adds to the smart appearance.

Another fabric may be used as the center panel that is covered by the mattress, e.g. muslin (calico), sheeting, or any other spare fabric.

A GATHERED DUST RUFFLE (VALANCE)

Braids, borders, fan edgings, or other trimmings should all be applied after the strips have been joined together.

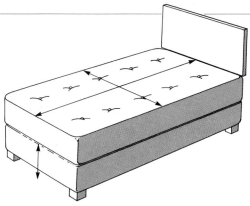

1 To calculate the center panel, measure the length and width of the bed allowing ½ in (12 mm) seam allowance on three sides and 2 in (5 cm) hem allowance at the headboard end. Cut out the panel. Cut a gentle curve at the corners, using a saucer or similar object. Machine stitch a double hem at the headboard end.

2 For the skirt depth, measure from the top of the box spring or, if there is none, from the bed frame to the floor (exclude the depth of the mattress), add ½ in (12 mm) seam allowance along one long edge and 2 in (5 cm) for a double hem along the other. The length will be twice the bed length plus the width and 2 in (5 cm) for hems at either end. Calculate the amount of gathers. This will depend on the fabric. Fine voiles or lace should be three times the length and heavier fabrics may only require one-and-a-half to two times the length. Cut out strips to this length, and join with a French seam.

3 Calculate the amount of border, ribbon, or trim by measuring the hemline edge of the skirt (valance) plus 1 in (2.5 cm) allowance for both ends.

4 Make the hem by turning back ½ in (12 mm), and then 1½ in (4 cm). Pin, press, and machine stitch with matching thread.

5 Make a mark with tailor's chalk at the center point of the foot end of the center panel and halfway between this and the bedhead on either side. Divide the skirt (valance) strip into four and mark. These reference points will ensure that the gathers are evenly spaced.

6 To gather the skirt, make two rows of gathering stitches, and pull up.

7 With the right sides together and the marks corresponding on the muslin (calico) panel and the skirt (valance), pin and machine stitch the skirt to the center panel.

8 Trim the seam and zigzag stitch to finish the raw edges.

9 If applying a trim, measure from the hemmed edge for the depth of the trimming. Mark a line all around. Pin the trimming to this line, and machine stitch in place using thread that matches the trimming.

Note that fan edges are generally put tight onto the bottom edge and can be pinned on before the hem is stitched. One line of stitching then attaches the trim and makes the hem.

10 To finish with binding, see page 92.

MAKING A TAILORED DUST RUFFLE (VALANCE)

Materials

skirt (valance) fabric
lining
matching thread
tailor's chalk
binding for the edge if desired

1 Make the center panel as for the gathered skirt (valance).

2 Cut strips to make up the skirt (valance) to the height of the bed, less the mattress, and allow ½ in (12 mm) seam along one long edge and a 2 in (5 cm) double hem along the other. For the length, measure twice the length of the bed plus the width at the foot end. Add 18 in (40 cm) for each corner pleat and 2 in (5 cm) seams at either end.

3 Join the strips, matching patterns if necessary. Neaten the raw edges or make French seams on delicate fabrics. Press.

4 Turn up the hem as for the gathered skirt (valance).

5 Starting at the pillow end, with right sides together, pin the skirt to the center panel, raw edges together, until you reach the corner as marked with tailor's chalk.

6 Repeat along the other side, then mark the center point of the remaining unpinned fabric strip. Mark the center of the frame of the panel, and join these two points. Pin outward to the corners as before.

7 The surplus fabric at the corners can now be formed into the inverted pleats. Remember to check the effect on the right side. The pleat itself should align with the corner mark.

8 Place the skirt (valance) on the bed frame under the mattress to check that the pleat is against the corner. Machine stitch all around to attach to the center panel.

Box-pleated Dust Ruffle (Valance)

Calculate the length of the skirt by measuring twice the length and width, and cutting out a strip three times this measurement. The depth is as for a gathered dust ruffle (valance).

Cut out and join the strips of fabric and hem. In box pleating, the spaces between the pleats are all equal. Each box and each space should, for example, be 4 in (10 cm), and the amount of turn-back on each pleat should be 2 in (5 cm).

Mark out the pleats with tailor's chalk, making sure that a pleat goes across each corner.

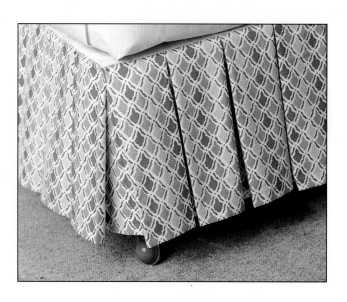

A F I T T E D B E D C O V E R

A fitted bedcover, with inverted pleats, especially when contrast-piped, is generally thought to have a tailored appearance, as it fits tightly over the bed hiding all the bedclothes, though if you use a duvet this may not be possible. With bolster cushions (see page 17) at either end, it can also serve in a sitting room as a sofa. In such cases a lightweight wool, or a fabric that is heavy enough not to crease, would be suitable, and in all cases make sure that the pattern runs down the skirt on all sides.

The bedcover is made in three pieces: the skirt, which can be pleated or gathered, the top panel, which is made to the same size as the muslin (calico) panel in the gathered dust ruffle (valance), and a fitted strip that goes around three sides of the mattress. The matching headboard cover is described on the next page.

1 Cut out and make up the skirt (valance) strips as for the pleated skirt (valance). Hem the bottom edge.

2 Cut out the center panel as for the gathered dust ruffle (valance), but this time using the main fabric. Hem the headboard end. (You may want the cover to wrap around the pillow or a bolster in which case extend the center panel by the required amount, see page 91, and hem the raw edges.)

3 To cut out the side strips, measure the depth of the mattress plus 1 in (2.5 cm) seam allowance, and cut two strips the length of the bed, and one for the foot, adding seam allowances. Sew the strips together with the shorter strip in the middle.

4 With right sides together, attach the side strips to the center panel, making sure the corner seams correspond to the marked corners on the center panel. Check for fit on the made-up bed before proceeding.

5 Join the skirt (valance) to the side strips as for the pleated dust ruffle (valance).

M a t e r i a l s

main fabric
piping if desired
matching thread

COVERING A HEADBOARD

*A*lthough headboards form only part of the bed, they are important. We lean up against them when reading and they help to coordinate with the color and mood of the room. Generally fully upholstered, they can also be loose-covered – the simpler the shape, the easier it is to sew.

Headboard covers generally fall into three categories: a plain slipcover, a boxed slipcover with piping, or some other trim, and an upholstered cover with piping and/or ruching. While it is relatively simple to make a plain slipcover, an upholstered cover is probably best left to a professional. A slipcover (loose cover) can be taken off and laundered, while the upholstered cover has to be dry cleaned.

Piping is the most common form of introducing a second color when covering a headboard. It is put around the outside edge of the gusset or approximately 4 in (10 cm) in, forming a border that follows the contours of the bedhead. If you are piping a fine rib or tweed with a contrast, make sure that the piping fabric is thin enough so that it forms a sharp line rather than a lumpy one.

Buttoning down in the same fabric as the piping gives a smart appearance as well as being practical. To remove the cover for cleaning, merely snip off the buttons and resew them in position when the cover is cleaned or washed.

M a t e r i a l s

main fabric
matching thread
fabric in a contrasting color for piping
paper for template (newspaper will be large enough)

1 Calculate the amount of fabric required by measuring the headboard and adding ½ in (12 mm) seam allowances all around. If the shape is not regular, make a paper template. Cut out the two pieces for the headboard cover. Cut a strip the width of the headboard and the length all around three sides plus seam allowances.

2 Mark where the headboard legs are to go on both panels.

3 Measure for the lengths of piping, and cut enough bias strips from the contrasting fabric to make up the piping. This should be applied along both gusset seams, so double the length.

4 Make up four ties (see page 20) for attaching the headboard cover to the bed.

5 With the right side facing, raw edges together, pin the piping around three sides of one panel, leaving the edge that will be nearest the mattress without piping. Baste (tack), then machine stitch in place using the zipper foot. Repeat for the other panel.

6 With right sides facing, pin the strip around one panel, and machine stitch in place. Notch the curves, and trim any corners. Check the fit.

7 Join the gusset to the other panel in the same way. Check the fit again, and press all seams.

8 Turn in ½ in (12 mm) along the open edge, and hem or bind with bias-cut fabric.

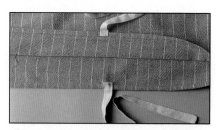

9 Attach one tie to each side of the cover at the marked points where the headboard legs will be.

A padded or quilted cover can be made by using ready-quilted fabric, or you can pad the cover with polyester batting (wadding) that is lockstitched (see page 33) to the fabric and then backed with a lining to hold it in place. You can use buttons for added emphasis. Sew the buttons through the three layers of fabric.

*T*HE *F*OUR *P*OSTER

*T*he four poster bed can be contemporary or romantic depending on the fabrics and trims used. Cotton, chintz, silk, velour, or lace and voile are all equally suitable.

Bed drapes can be highly complex or merely simple panels of fabric tied to the four posts. The components of bed drapes for a four poster include the side curtains, usually lined in a contrasting fabric, the roof, the back of the bed behind the headboard, and the valance running around the top. The roof, or "sunburst", of the bed is best left to the professionals. Alternatively, this space can be left open.

The bed drapes can be made with two side curtains, made as for window curtains (see page 32), and a gathered back or four curtains, generally of one width each, at each post. These curtains are not made to be drawn; they reveal the decorative upright post. The curtains at the head

end are held back with tiebacks, and those at the foot end are often left hanging free. It is better to make handsewn headings (see page 35), alternatively attach an inner valance that will cover a taped heading. This is done by using Velcro along the inside of the frame of the bed.

The back can be gathered by means of a curtain, two or three times the measured width of the back, that is slotted through a pole or rod and fixed by means of buttonholes or ties to the back of the bed, or possibly from two brackets on the wall. The bed headboard can then be positioned as normal.

The valance of the bed goes around three sides. The easiest way to attach it is by sticking Velcro all around the frame. The depth of the valance should be in proportion to the height of the bed and should follow the lines of any other window valances (pelmets).

SIMPLE BED DRAPES

The simplest form of bed drapes is to have a single strip of fabric draped over a short pole (approximately 12 in/30 cm long), which is attached to the ceiling or slotted into a bracket on the wall above the center of the bedhead.

The style is immensely popular possibly because it uses less fabric and takes up less room than a canopy (coronet fitting) while still giving a stylish finish and extra glamor to the bedroom. The fabrics used should coordinate with those of the window curtains or the bedcovers, or a soft voile could be used for a romantic effect.

MAKING SIMPLE BED DRAPES

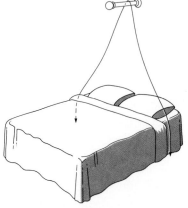

Materials

main fabric
lining if desired
short pole or bracket
tiebacks, tassels, or braid
cleats for the tiebacks

1 Attach the pole to the ceiling or wall. If it is a wall attachment, the fabric can be slotted onto the pole by means of a casing.

2 Measure from the floor up and over the pole and down to the other side of the bed; measure the length of the pole and allow one or two widths of fabric. Allow an extra 6 in (15 cm) on the length if you plan to make a casing. Be generous with the length of fabric.

3 Make up a long strip of fabric to the required length and width.

4 Make up a length of lining to exactly the same measurements. Place the two strips right sides together and pin all around the outside. Machine stitch together with a seam allowance of ½ in (12 mm). Leave an opening on one side.

5 Turn the fabric right side out, press and slipstitch the opening closed. If you are making a casing, fold the strip in half with the right sides facing out, and machine stitch across 3 in (8 cm) down from the fold.

6 Hang the drapes over the pole, so there are equal lengths on either side, or thread the casing onto it.

7 Tie the drapes back on either side with a tieback or tassels.

8 To secure the fabric along the pole you can unobtrusively place a thumb tack (drawing pin) through the pole and fabric.

MAKING CANOPY (CORONET-FIXED) DRAPES

This method is ideal because the curtain rod (track) is already fitted inside the half-moon shape. The canopy (coronet) is fixed to the wall above the bedhead with angle irons.

Generally a canopy (coronet) has a well-gathered, inexpensive back curtain. Soft unlined fabric looks simple and pretty as the curtaining, if used very full. It can also be taken down and washed. Lawn and other gossamer-thin fabrics are the perfect choice.

The two side curtains are made like a normal window curtain, either plain lined, or interlined.

Generally if they are lined, the fabric is the same as the back of the bed. If this is voile, separate side curtains will have to be made with separate headings. These are held back in a variety of ways – tiebacks in the same or contrasting fabric, ropes with or without tassels, soft bows, rosettes, or brass holdbacks.

The sides of the curtains can be extravagantly ruffled (frilled), single or double, with piping, or without. Fringes are best kept small, or use a fan-edge trim. A 1 in (2.5 cm) binding is often the most effective.

<table>
<tr><td>

Materials

main fabric
canopy (coronet) and angle irons
cleats to hold the tiebacks
tiebacks (see page 42)
lining fabric (if necessary)
heading tape
curtain hooks, rings, or Velcro

</td></tr>
</table>

1 Fix the canopy (coronet) on the wall above the bed at the desired height.

2 Measure the distance from the fitting to the floor to calculate the length of the curtain. Add extra fabric for the sweep to the side of the bed, usually about 20 in (50 cm). A simple way to do this is to tie string to the corona and drape it. Measure the length of string to estimate the desired drop of fabric. The widths of the side curtains should be about one to one-and-a-half times the measured width, depending on the thickness of the fabric. You may decide on three times for very fine fabric. For the back curtain, measure to the floor, and allow two widths of fabric for a single bed and three for a double. (If the fabric is not in decorator-fabric widths, then use more widths.)

3 Join the seams as for curtains, and make up with a gathered heading tape (see page 31).

Small swags (see page 48) as a valance look effective and elegant, especially in soft lace. A feathery fringe about 4 in (10 cm) deep is easily applied, and looks wonderful, especially if it coordinates with the fabric.

4 If the canopy frame (coronet) itself needs to be covered, make a valance for it. The width measurement is that of the half-moon shape, the depth should be in proportion. To judge this, drape a piece of fabric from the top of the fitting and stand back to observe the effect. Cut out the fabric to the desired measurements plus seam allowances and make as for a curtain valance (see page 39). Attach to the fitting with Velcro.

TABLES

STYLES AND FABRICS

The simplest and least complicated soft furnishing project is to make your own table linen. An elegant rectangular tablecloth is a piece of fabric, hemmed around all sides. The napkins can be made in the same fabric as the cloth or in a coordinating fabric and the edges embellished with different trims and stitches. Table runners are another traditional idea for using fabric on the table without its being overpowering.

The style of the tablecloth adds an important flavor to the room. A cheerful checked cloth with napkins picked out in one of the colors, and a bright floral arrangement, suits an informal kitchen/dining room. A floor-length crisp linen cloth with lilies and candles is the epitome of elegance. Side tables also provide many options. They can be simple with a short, businesslike co-ordinating cloth, or dressed in elaborate fabric swags. A side table is often covered with a frilly cloth or perhaps two – an undercloth that drapes along the floor, and a smaller cloth with an interesting edging, or one that is made up in embroidered fabric.

FABRIC

The choice of fabric for tablecloths depends on what the table is going to be used for. If there will be food and drink served on the table, then obviously a fabric that washes well and looks crisp and smart is the best choice. For display tablecloths, anything goes. There is no reason why you cannot use a decorative shawl or a piece of embroidery such as crewelwork over an undercloth that will hide the legs of the table.

The cloth can be edged with braid and tassels, or the hemline can be padded or shaped in a scallop or zigzag.

Table napkins are the simplest project of all. At their most basic they are squares of fabric with a line of stitching that either turns in the raw edges or is frayed away to produce fringes.

When deciding on color, a good place to start is with your china. If you favor all-white dinner settings, then the tablecloth color needs to be a textured or pale fabric with some interest in the form of embroidery or pattern. With bright colored china, the fabric can be chosen to coordinate or contrast – checks and stripes for a country look, chintz florals for a more traditional style, and damask and linen for elegance.

DECIDING ON THE STYLE

The style of table linen does not have to be limited to covering the top and part way down the legs. A beautiful old pine or oak table with a well-worn top can have place mats or a small square cloth placed on an angle so that only the center of the table and the sides are covered. For a less attractive table, with ugly stained legs, the cloth should go right to the floor, although this style has to be chosen with care. If you have small children, the cloth may become wrapped around someone's leg and be pulled off.

For side tables, there are many different options. If the table isn't large enough for the space, you can cut a larger circle of Masonite (chipboard) and secure that to the top. The undercloth should drop right to the floor, and the top cloth can come halfway down, or be square or fitted so that it acts rather like a cap to secure the undercloth.

In the bedroom, romance can take over, and you may feel that you need the opulence of masses of fabric. Dressing tables can be covered with ruffled cloths that are then covered over with ruched top skirts or swags of cloth around the edge, rather like the swags in window dressing (see page 48). To protect the top of any cloth that isn't changed regularly, have glass cut to fit. This also acts as a weight to prevent the cloth from being pulled off.

If you limit yourself to place mats, then you might consider interlining them with a heat-resistant fabric to protect your table.

This well-chosen, ribbon-patterned, glazed cotton fabric makes a key feature of a small side table. The circular cloth is simply made without any trimmings. The fullness of the fabric is luxurious enough on its own.

THE BASIC TABLECLOTH

*T*his is the basis for most tablecloths for a square or rectangular table. Napkins and place mats are made in the same way, but on a different scale.

Before you begin, you need to decide on the style, particularly the length. Use an old sheet or another tablecloth to see the best effect. If the table legs are attractive, then plan for the cloth to finish halfway down the legs. A good length for the cloth to hang is just above a chair seat.

Materials

fabric
matching thread
decorative edging

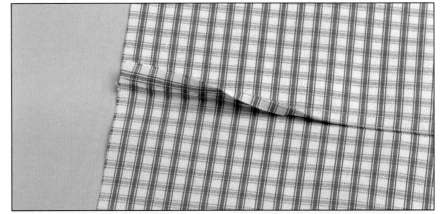

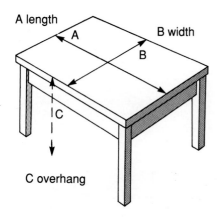

A length
A
B width
B
C
C overhang

1 Measure the width and the length of the table. Decide on the overhang and add twice this to the width and length. Add on a 2 in (5 cm) hem allowance or none at all if you plan to add a purchased decorative edging.

2 If the table is very large, you will probably have to join widths of fabric. Avoid a seam down the center. Use the full width of the fabric on the center of the table, and add extra widths at the sides. Remember to add on for the seam allowance.

3 Cut out the fabric, and join any widths with flat-fell seams, as follows. With right sides together, machine stitch the two pieces of fabric together. Press the seam allowances to one side. Trim the underlying seam to ¼ in (6 mm) and fold the top allowance

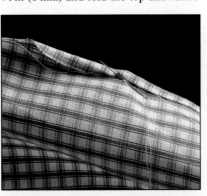

4 The hemming will depend on the fabric. If you are using fine fabrics, then roll the hemline, and hand stitch. Machine stitch a line of stitches ¼ in (6 mm) from the raw edge. Using your thumb and forefinger, roll the fabric to enclose the raw edge, and hem by hand.

back over it, turning in the raw edge to enclose the trimmed one. Pin and press before machine sewing along the folded edge through all layers. This seam shows topstitching on the right side, so load the bobbin with matching thread.

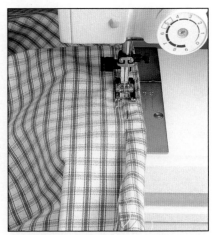

5 For a machine stitched hem, turn under 1 in (2.5 cm) twice and pin. You can miter the corners (see page 33), or overlap them neatly. Press well before stitching.

Below are three simple ideas for trimming a kitchen tablecloth: a plain border in matching color; a border in a coordinating design, and an inset strip in white.

TABLE NAPKINS AND PLACE MATS

Materials

fabric
matching thread

1 Decide on the dimensions of your napkins. They should always be square. They will look skimpy if they are any smaller than 12 in (30 cm) square. Use the width of the fabric and cut an equal number from this, allowing for a 1 in (2.5 cm) hem allowance. Make sure you cut them out on the straight of the grain.

2 For place mats, use your large dinner plates as a guide to the finished size. Allow at least 3 in (8 cm) top and bottom, and 4 in (10 cm) either side of the plate.

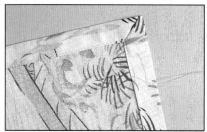

3 Hem the napkins and place mats as for the tablecloth. Because they are laundered so frequently, make sure you catch in the corners when you machine stitch them.

4 To fringe the napkin edges, machine stitch a row of stitches 1 in (2.5 cm) in from the edge.

5 Using a pin, pull out the threads until the fringe reaches the line of stitching.

DECORATIVE EDGINGS FOR
NAPKINS AND PLACE MATS

When you hem napkins and place mats, the machine line of stitching can be used as a decorative edging too. Set the machine to sew satin stitch and choose a contrasting thread. This looks best on floral chintz fabrics when you pick out one of the colors in the pattern for the thread. Sew the line of satin stitches along the hemmed edge, about ½ in (12 mm) in from the edge.

Commercial ribbons and narrow braids sewn ½ in (12 mm) in from the edge are another decorative possibility. Choose a matching thread and machine stitch along the very edge of the braid. Check that you haven't missed anywhere because laundering will cause the braid to loosen if it isn't secured properly.

The satin-stitched hem on place mat and napkin is both practical and decorative. Many fabrics are printed with figurative scenes or other motifs and these provide a readymade theme for a set of place mats when carefully cut.

A LINED CLOTH

For a formal tablecloth, or for the versatility of a reversible cloth, you can add a lining. The edges are bound with ribbon or a bias strip providing an additional decorative touch.

Materials

main fabric
lining fabric*
matching thread
ribbon or bias strips cut from a coordinating fabric

* Choose a fabric similar in fiber content and weight.

1 Measure and cut out the fabric and lining to the same dimensions adding a seam allowance of ½ in (12 mm) all around. Join any widths where necessary.

2 Press the seams open and iron out any wrinkles.

3 Lay the two pieces of fabric with wrong sides together, and pin around the edges. If the cloth is very large, you will need to lock-stitch the layers together (see page 33).

4 Baste (tack) by machine around all four sides.

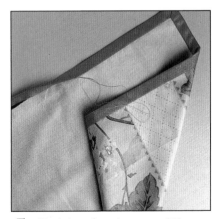

5 Bind the edges (see page 92). Take care to use invisible hand sewing when finishing off, if the cloth is to be reversible.

*A*PPLIQUÉD *T*ABLECLOTH AND *N*APKINS

Appliqué is a versatile soft-furnishing technique. It can be as simple as cutting out a rose from a patterned fabric, and sewing it onto a plain fabric (this is known as *broderie perse*), or you can build up cut-out fabric shapes to make a figurative picture.

The charm of appliqué lies in its simplicity, and in the way it links various items together. So if you appliqué a bunch of flowers in the center of a tablecloth, you could pick out a smaller flower from the design and appliqué one in the corner of each napkin.

The design can be made from the one layer of fabric or the motif can be padded with fiberfill batting (synthetic wadding) to add a quilted effect. The fabrics chosen for appliqué should be the same weight as the background fabric to ensure even wear but if you find a design you really like in a delicate fabric, then use an iron-on interfacing to strengthen it.

Double-sided fusible webbing is another material that makes appliqué simple. The webbing is ironed onto the wrong side of the motif, then the paper backing is removed, and the other side is ironed onto the right side of the main fabric. This holds the motif securely in position while you finish the raw edges with some form of decorative stitching.

——— B R O D E R I E   P E R S E   T A B L E C L O T H ———

Materials

main fabric
patterned fabric with distinctive design*
lightweight iron-on interfacing or double-sided fusible webbing
thread to match one of the predominant colors in the chosen motif
dressmaker's chalk

* Large flowers and leaves, animals or scenes in an even-weave fabric.

1 Measure and cut out the tablecloth and napkins (see pages 106 to 108), and finish the edges. Press well.

2 Decide on the parts of the pattern that you are going to use, and cut them out leaving a 1 in (2.5 mm) allowance all around. Arrange the motifs on the tablecloth until you are happy with the look. Mark the position with dressmaker's chalk. Remember that the extra layer of fabric and lines of stitching will raise the tablecloth in places making it a difficult surface to

put glasses on, so try not to place the motifs around the table edge. The best position is in the center or at the hemline. An appliquéd hemline is ideal for a circular cloth (see page 113).

3 Iron the interfacing or fusible webbing to the wrong side of the motifs. Cut away any excess fabric with sharp scissors.

4 If you are using interfacing, place the motif in position, trying to keep the grain running in the same direction as that of the tablecloth. Carefully cut the interfacing away around the edge of the motif, and pin onto the right side of the tablecloth. Baste (tack) the motif.

5 If using fusible webbing, remove the paper backing from the motif and iron in position using a damp cloth with a hot iron, or follow manufacturer's instructions.

6 Using a thread that picks out one of the motif colors, zigzag around the shape to cover the raw edges.

7 Using a satin stitch, machine stitch around the edges once more to finish (see page 108).

Complex Designs

If you are working with a number of cutout motifs, you will need to arrange them until you are happy with the result before sewing. Mark the positions with dressmaker's chalk. Sew the background motifs first, and cut away any fabric that will be covered by subsequent motifs. This reduces the thickness of the layers.

M AKING A C IRCULAR C LOTH

*C*loths on a round table hang in deep folds and so you need to choose the fabric to suit the table. A floor-length cloth made from crisp cotton or linen will be the appropriate weight for a bedside table. For an opulent living room with a larger round table, you might choose a heavy wool or kilim pattern. On a large table, the fabric needs to be heavier to hold the folds well.

On small bedside tables or occasional tables in living rooms, a short square overcloth placed on top of a full-length round one works well. Try a combination of plain and patterned fabric or add a lace runner (overcloth). Alternatively, make a short round runner (overcloth) with an appliquéd hem, as described on the next page. The appliqué motifs can be taken from scraps from the curtain fabric or other draperies in the room.

Materials

main fabric
lining or backing fabric
paper for pattern*
thin fiberfill batting (synthetic wadding)†
binding or other decorative edging
pencil
length of string
thumb tack (drawing pin)

* Newspapers or lining paper.
† To emphasize the weight, you can pad the cloth, particularly if the table is made from precious wood that is easily marked. This will make frequent washing less convenient. You might decide to use a separate piece of padding under the cloth to protect the table.

A diameter

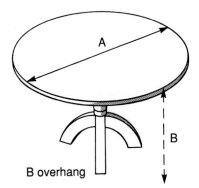

A

B

B overhang

1 Measure the diameter of the table, then decide on the depth of the overhang. Add twice the overhang to the diameter. Include a ½ in (12 mm) hem allowance.

2 To cut out a square of fabric with each side the diameter of the cloth, you will need to join some

widths first. Lay one complete width out flat and, matching any pattern, join part widths on either side along the selvage. Machine stitch the seams and press them open. Snip the selvage to release any tension.

3 Fold the fabric into four.

4 To make a paper pattern, make up a piece of paper the size of the folded fabric. Make a quarter-circle pattern the diameter of the finished cloth (see page 15), and cut out the pattern.

5 Pin the pattern to the folded fabric around all the edges. Cut along the curved line through all layers.

6 If you are lining the cloth, cut a piece of lining using the paper pattern again.

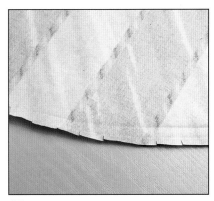

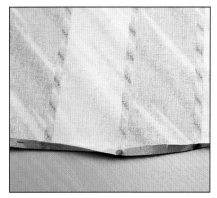

10 If you are lining the cloth, after step 7 turn under ½ in (12 mm) around both circles and pin. Do not press. Place the two layers with wrong sides together on a flat surface and lockstitch together if necessary (see page 33).

11 Slipstitch the folds of the hems together all around. Press the cloth but not at the edges.

7 Cut notches about ¼ in (6 mm) deep in the raw edge of the circle all around the circumference at 1 in (2.5 cm) intervals. This helps the hem to lie flat. Cut notches in the lining too.

8 Turn under ¼ in (6 mm) all around the cloth for the hem. Press and then turn under for another ¼ in (6 mm). Press again.

9 Machine stitch or hem by hand.

A circular cloth can take any of the decorative trimmings. Attach fringe just above the hem so that it rests on the floor when the cloth is on the table. Another hemline that suits a circular cloth is a shaped hem (see page 115).

An Appliquéd Hem

This is time consuming but it looks very effective as a runner (overcloth) on a pretty side table. If you decide that you do not want to appliqué the entire hem, you can bind or hem those raw edges that are left exposed between the motifs, as described and illustrated below.

Materials

main fabric
appliqué shapes
iron-on interfacing
matching thread*

* Pick out one of the colors in the motif.

1 Cut out the tablecloth. Do not add a hem allowance.

2 Cut out the appliqué motifs and back with iron-on interfacing.

3 Plan the positioning of the motifs around the hemline, so that they just touch the raw edge. In some places the shapes themselves might overlap. Pin and baste (tack).

4 Zigzag-stitch the shapes in place, then finish off with satin stitch (see page 108).

5 Carefully cut away any parts of the main fabric that show between the motifs, so that part of the appliqué motif protrudes beyond the edge of the cloth.

6 Finish any raw edges of the hemline with binding or roll the hem by hand (see page 106).

DECORATIVE EDGINGS

The trimming or decoration on a tablecloth is important to the style and mood of the table setting. A heavy, richly colored damask cloth is improved with a wide bound edge in a contrasting color. A dressing table suits a ruffled trimming – either single or double or even bound in a contrasting binding. If the edge of a circular cloth is faced, then scallops or zigzags can be shaped along the hem. Appliqué is also used to finish an edge on a small runner (overcloth) (see page 113). This has the advantage that any weight around the hemline makes the cloth hang better.

A small circular table in the bedroom or living room can take a gathered skirt. This is made in much the same way as a gathered dust ruffle (valance) (see page 95), and the cloth can be held in place with a piece of glass cut to fit, which also provides an easy-to-clean surface.

A RUFFLED, BOUND, CIRCULAR TABLECLOTH

If a piece of fabric is gathered down the center for its length, a ruffle will be created on both sides of the machine stitching. It should not be too wide or the top part will flop forward and spoil the effect, or too stiff or it will not gather smoothly. A crisp fabric is the best choice.

Materials

main fabric
binding
matching thread

---

1 Measure for the tablecloth; cut out, and hem (see page 112).

2 To calculate the length of fabric for the ruffle, measure the circumference of the finished cloth and double it. The width should be in proportion to the cloth, say between 2 in (5 cm) and 5 in (13 cm) finished width. Add a hem allowance of 1 in (2.5 cm) if you are not binding the edges. Join strips to make a circle of fabric.

3 Calculate the amount of binding and join the required number of strips.

4 Bind both edges of the ruffle (see page 92). Press.

5 Fold the tablecloth into four and mark the hem at each quarter. Divide the ruffle into four equal lengths, and mark with pins.

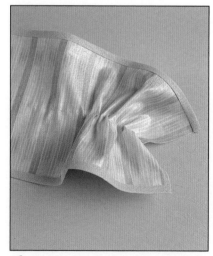

6 Run a length of gathering stitches down the center of the ruffle. Match the pins on the ruffle with those on the cloth, and gather up the stitches to fit evenly around the edge. Pin along the line of stitches, so that the base edge of the ruffle aligns with the finished hem.

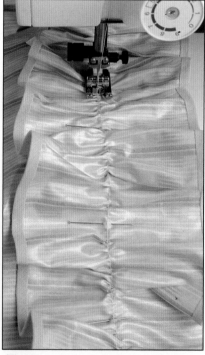

7 Topstitch the ruffle to the cloth.

Another option is to offset the gathering stitches so the top part of the ruffle is only one third of the total depth (see opposite).

Facing a Circular Hem

If you attach a facing to a tablecloth, you can then either pad it to help the cloth hang better or when you sew along the hem line you can make a scallop or a line of zigzags.

Materials

main fabric
matching thread
paper for template
dressmaker's chalk or pencil

---

1 Measure for the tablecloth as before. Allow extra in the same fabric for the facing. Cut out the top cloth, and fold into quarters.

2 Using the cloth as a template, make a paper pattern for the facing. Cut a facing for a quarter of the cloth adding 1 in (2.5 cm) seam allowance. The facing should follow the edge of the cloth and be at least 8 in (20 cm) deep.

3 Cut out four facings and with right sides together, join the four facings into a complete circle, allowing ½ in (12 mm) seam allowance. Turn under and machine stitch a single hem along the inner edge. Press.

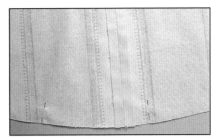

4 With right sides together and raw edges matching, pin the facing around the edge of the cloth.

5 Using the paper pattern as a guide, decide on the shape of the hemline. Ensure that there are equal spaces between scallops or zigzag points.

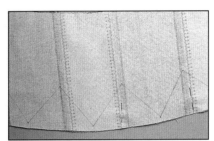

6 Transfer the shapes to the facing using a pencil or dressmaker's chalk.

7 Machine stitch around the shaped hem ¼ in (6 mm) in from the edge. Trim the seam and clip the curves.

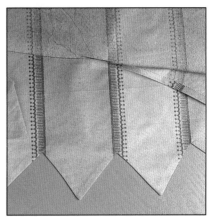

8 Turn right sides out and press. Hand sew the facing to the cloth with blind stitches.

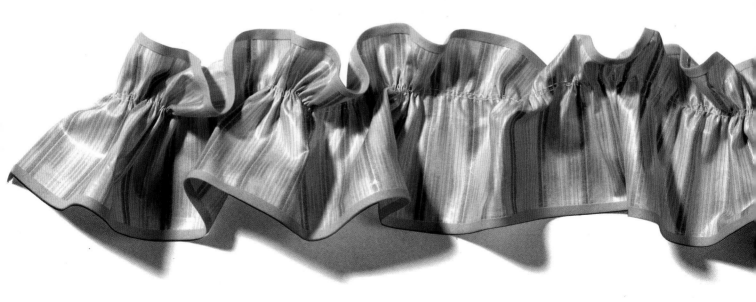

LAMPSHADES

LAMPSHADES

*L*ampshades are significant accessories in a room. It is important when choosing a shade to respect the style of the room and the lamp base. There is a wide variety of shades (see below) available from specialist suppliers.

When choosing the color for shades, consider what purpose the light is going to serve – whether it is to be purely decorative or merely functional for reading or sewing. Paler colors are more suitable for functional lighting because they shed a brighter light. Nonetheless most colors are acceptable if they fit into your decorative scheme, though blue and white often give a cold light.

Lampshades can be made from many different types of fabric – fine to medium weight, close weave silks (such as Thai, shantung, or honan), lightweight cotton, chintz, or rayon dupion. Avoid fabric with a loose weave. All shades are enhanced by balloon linings. These are fitted inside the frame. They hide the ribs (struts) and prevent the bulb from showing through the cover fabric. If they are pale, they reflect a considerable amount of light. Linings can also enrich the colors of the shade. Suitable linings for silk shades are crêpe de Chine or crêpe-backed satin, and cotton poplin for cotton shades.

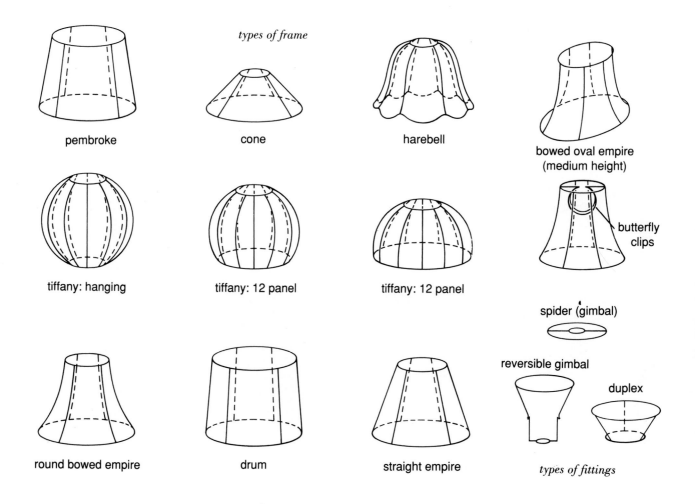

types of frame

pembroke

cone

harebell

bowed oval empire
(medium height)

butterfly clips

tiffany: hanging

tiffany: 12 panel

tiffany: 12 panel

spider (gimbal)

reversible gimbal

duplex

round bowed empire

drum

straight empire

types of fittings

ELASTICIZED TIFFANY SHADE

Tiffany-shaped shades are the simplest and quickest to make. As the cover is elasticized around the top and bottom, it can be easily removed for washing. Suitable fabrics are lightweight curtain fabrics, dress fabrics, lace, voile, and eyelet (broderie anglaise). The translucent fabrics are sometimes enhanced by colored linings. The most suitable frames for this method are shown on page 118.

The "Tiffany" shade (left) has a colored lining underneath a spotted voile and is trimmed with an eyelet ruffle (broderie anglaise frill).

Materials

Tiffany frame, pendant fitting
cover fabric, spotted voile or similar lightweight cotton
lining fabric, cotton lawn
eyelet ruffle (broderie anglaise frill)
narrow elastic
sewing thread to match cover fabric
glass-headed pins
soft pencil or dressmaker's chalk

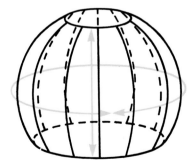

1 To calculate the amount of fabric required for the Tiffany shade, measure one rib (strut) and add 3 in (8 cm) for turnings. Then measure the circumference of the shade at the widest point and add 1 in (2.5 cm) for the seam allowance.

2 File any sharp surfaces on the frame. There is no need to bind it in this instance because the cover is not to be sewn to the frame.

3 Cut out the cover and lining fabric on the straight of grain. With right sides facing, join the short edges together and machine stitch a ½ in (12 mm) seam on both cover and lining fabric. Trim and press the seam open. Place the lining inside the cover with both seams matching and wrong sides of fabric facing.

4 To make casings for the elastic along the top and bottom edges, turn and press a ½ in (12 mm) hem twice (with both cover and lining together) and machine stitch, leaving a small gap in each hem to insert the elastic.

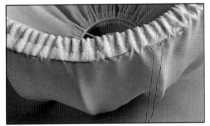

5 Place the cover over the frame and insert the elastic in the casings until you get the desired fit. Mark the elastic where it is to be joined. While the cover is on the frame, mark the line where the trim is to be placed with basting (tacking) thread or dressmaker's chalk. This should be on or just above the bottom ring. Remove the cover from the frame.

6 Cut the required length of 2½–3 in (6–8 cm) ruffle (frill) – the circumference of the base. Join the ends with a flat-fell seam (see page 106), and topstitch the ruffle (frill) to the cover along the trim line. Remove basting (tacking) thread.

7 Sew the ends of elastic together in both casings and position the cover over the frame.

CLASSIC SHADES

The classic shade described here is made out of lightweight cotton curtain fabric, self-edged in the same fabric top and bottom, and balloon-lined in cotton. This particular style of shade looks attractive in a bedroom and is appropriate for side lamps and ceiling lights.

Materials

Pembroke or cone frame, spider (gimbal) fitting
cover fabric, such as lightweight curtaining (allow enough for pattern repeat and bias strips)
lining fabric, cotton poplin
½ in (12 mm)-wide lampshade binding tape
upholstery thread
glass-headed pins
soft pencil or dressmaker's chalk
fabric adhesive

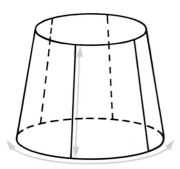

1 To calculate the amount of fabric required for the cover and lining, measure halfway around the circumference of the lower ring of the frame and add 2 in (5 cm) on either side. Measure the height of one rib (strut) and add 2 in (5 cm) extra at the top and bottom. Cut out the fabric – two pieces for both the cover and lining – with the straight of grain running from top-to-bottom. If using patterned fabric, match your pattern at this stage before cutting out. If the fabric you choose seems too light, you can stiffen it with spray-on fabric stiffener or, for a crisp effect, iron on a heavy interfacing.

2 Take the plastic-coated frame, check any rough surfaces and file. The frame should then be taped to provide a base for stitching. Calculate the amount of tape by allowing twice the circumference of the top and bottom ring and twice the length of two vertical ribs (struts). Cut equal lengths of binding tape (1 yard/1 meter). Bind the top and bottom rings followed by the two side ribs (struts), opposite one another, but without the fitting attached.

3 To tape the rings, start at a rib (strut), take the leading end up from inside and over the ring and rib (strut) at an angle. Bind the tape around this junction in a figure eight.

4 Continue binding around the ring with the tape at a slight angle, ensuring the binding is very tight, and there are no ridges in it. Bind a figure eight around all ribs (struts).

5 When joining a new length of tape, trim the end close to the ring, moisten the end of the new piece, and tuck it under the old end.

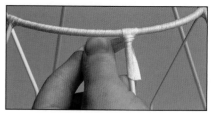

6 To finish the binding, secure the end around the initial rib (strut), bind the side ribs (struts) in the same way, bringing the leading end down over the top ring and rib (strut). There must be no movement in the binding as this would cause the shade to sag.

7 Take one piece of ironed cover fabric and crease it down the center on the straight of grain. Place the straight grain wrong side down along a central rib (strut) with the 2 in (5 cm) excess top and bottom. Pin the fabric to half the frame, keeping the crease on the center rib (strut) at all times until the material is taut across the frame, and all the wrinkles have been removed.

8 Mark the position of the ribs (struts) on the fabric with pencil dots at the top and bottom, and draw lines down the two outer ribs (struts), marking the position of the top and bottom rings with short horizontal lines. Remove the fabric from the frame.

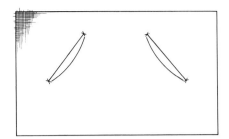

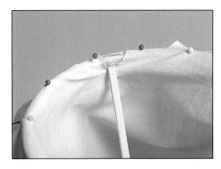

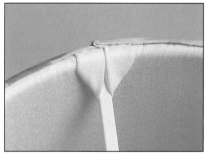

9 Prepare the lining in exactly the same way. As the balloon lining goes inside the frame, measure the difference between the outer and inner circumference of the rings and alter the pencil markings accordingly, then join these inner marks at top and bottom with an inwardly curving line on each side, as shown in the diagram above. This establishes the balloon effect later on.

10 Remove the binding from the two vertical ribs (struts) as this was done only to provide a base for pinning and measuring the fabric.

11 Machine stitch the two pieces of cover fabric with right sides together down the side pencil markings.

12 Reinforce the seams by putting a line of fabric adhesive on the outside of the stitches and iron until dry and hard. Trim off excess fabric from the seams, as close to the stitches as possible.

13 Machine stitch and trim the lining in the same way but use a double line of stitches instead of adhesive as a reinforcement. Pencil mark the position of the ribs (struts) on the stitched pieces of fabric.

14 Turn the cover right side out and place it over the frame, positioning the seams over the bound ribs (struts). Pin the cover to the rings (top ring first), until all the slack has been taken up and the cover is as tight as possible. Oversew along the top and bottom rings with a double thickness of upholstery thread. Trim off excess fabric from top and bottom as close to the stitches as possible.

15 Position the lining inside the frame, matching seams, and pin as for the cover, cutting the fabric down by the fitting, so it sits neatly around it. The lining must also be tight. Oversew as for the cover, keeping the stitches on the outside of the rings.

16 To finish the fitting, cut a strip of lining on the bias (see page 122), 4 × 1 in (10 × 2.5 cm), fold lengthwise into three, press, and position under the fitting to cover the hole in the lining. Stitch the two ends to the outside of the top ring. Trim off all excess fabric from the top and bottom rings.

17 To self-edge the shade, cut two strips of cover fabric on the bias the length of the top and bottom rings and 1 in (2.5 cm) wide. Fold into three lengthwise and press. Glue a strip to the top ring, stretching it as you work around, hiding all stitches. Overlap the ends and turn under ¼ in (6 mm) to finish.

BOWED EMPIRE SHADES

Bowed empire shades are a timeless shape and are ideal for living rooms. The bowed candle shades look especially attractive coupled on either side of a dressing table in a bedroom. They suit curved bases, such as brass, marble, and alabaster, as the shape can be reflected in the shade. The frames come in all sizes and are appropriate for both standard shades and candle shades. They can be round, oval, with a collar at the top or a band at the bottom, or even with a scalloped top. (See frames on page 118.)

The bowed effect of the frame shows a silk cover off to its best advantage. A perfect finishing trim is a self-edging in silk with bias strips together with a layer of narrow braid glued to the edge of the strips.

Bias Strips

To cut bias strips, first fold the selvage so that it is parallel with the crosswise grain. Press or mark this diagonal fold line with a soft pencil or dressmaker's chalk. This is your first cutting line.

To join strips, place the ends together so the fabric looks like a V. Press seams open and trim.

Materials

oval bowed empire frame,
duplex fitting
cover fabric, such as Thai silk
lining material, crêpe de Chine
narrow braid
pattern paper
upholstery thread
½ in (12 mm) lampshade binding tape
sewing thread to match cover and lining
glass-headed pins
soft pencil
fabric adhesive

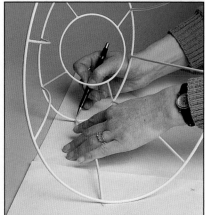

1 For bowed shades the fabric has to be cut on the bias to give it more elasticity to fit around the curve (bow). A paper pattern is used to calculate the amount of fabric. To make a pattern from the frame, fold the pattern paper at right angles and crease. Using a pencil, draw a line along the crease. Place the center rib (strut) on the long side of the shade along the crease, and roll over two further ribs (struts) on either side, making sure there is at least 2½ in (6 cm) of paper on either side of the second one. Mark the position at the top and bottom of all five ribs (struts) on the paper, and draw a line joining top and bottom of the two outer ones. Draw a cutting line 2 in (5 cm) below the bottom rib (strut) marks. Cut out.

2 Pin the pattern to the cover fabric, edge-to-edge, and cut out two pieces this way for the cover. Mark the top corners of the fabric with a pencil so the same sides can be matched at a later stage.

3 The next steps in preparing the cover and lining are the same as for the classic shade (see page 120). It is important to note when stretching the cover fabric onto the frame that it is tightened across to the side ribs (struts) before the bottom ring, so the bowed effect of the shade is not lost. Keep stretching and repinning until the cover is taut.

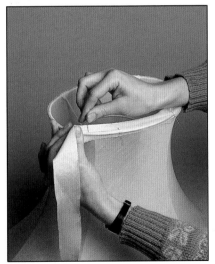

4 Cut bias strips for the edging (see left). Position a strip on the top ring by stretching it around and pinning it at intervals. Do the same on the bottom ring. Mark where the two ends are to be joined and machine stitch together with a double layer of stitches. Trim the seam and press open.

5 Fold the bias strip in three lengthwise, and press. Pin and whip (oversew) the bottom layer of the bias strip to the rings. Pull down the rest of the trim to cover all the stitching. This should fit tightly over the stitching. If there is any bagginess, secure it with adhesive. This method for self-edging gives the neatest finish.

6 Glue on a layer of braid flush with the self-edging. It is often attractive to have two layers of braid, perhaps incorporating another color from the decorative scheme of the room.

There is a large selection of upholstery braids, fringes and tassels in a wide range of colors suitable for lampshades.

PLEATED SHADES

*P*leated lampshades are a popular choice for ceramic bases, converted Chinese vases, and even tall brass candlesticks. They have a sophisticated appearance and give a gentle diffused light when the lamp is lit. There are many types of pleating, but one of the simplest and most effective ways is to knife pleat. Suggested fabrics are lightweight silks and fine cotton chintzes. Check the effect of the pleats before you decide, as the pleating may ruin a fabric pattern or not allow enough light through. Choose a frame that is not too graduated, such as a straight empire, drum, or pembroke (see page 118). Self-edging is a neat finish for these shades, or attach cotton or silk fringes. The shade in the photograph is covered with a shantung silk and finished with a cotton fan-edged trim.

Materials

straight empire frame, spider (gimbal) fitting
cover fabric, silk or floral chintz
silk trim
½ in (12 mm) lampshade binding tape
glass-headed pins
upholstery thread
sewing thread to match trim
soft pencil
fabric adhesive

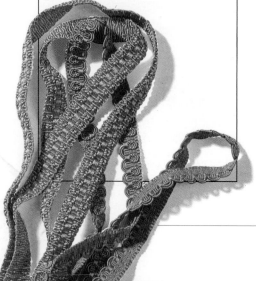

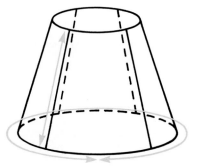

1 The amount of fabric needed for the pleated cover is three-and-a-half times the circumference of the base times the height of the rib (strut), plus 1½ in (4 cm) extra top and bottom. The widths of fabric should be cut on the straight and when cutting out the fabric, draw a pencil line 1½ in (4 cm) down from the top on the right side of the fabric. This is the pleat line. Remove all selvages and overcast (oversew) the raw edges to prevent fraying.

2 Establish the size of the pleats by dividing the base measurement by an average pleat size, say ½ in (12 mm). Count the number of gaps between the ribs (struts) and divide the pleat number by this for the number of pleats between each two ribs (struts).

3 Prepare and bind the frame as on page 120.

4 Start pleating by pinning the fabric to the frame at the bottom of a rib (strut), and working around the frame from left to right. As the pleat size is ½ in (12 mm), measure 1½ in (4 cm) from the head of the pleat and turn back 1 in (2.5 cm), leaving a pleat of ½ in (12 mm). Pin this pleat and continue pleating and pinning to the next rib (strut), always keeping the penciled pleat line in the same position on the bottom ring. Make sure there are no gaps between the pleats; gaps give an unsightly and irregular appearance when the light is on.

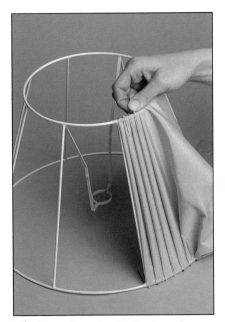

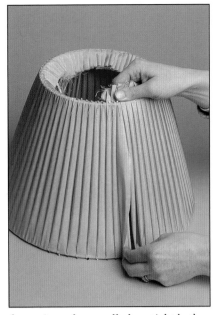

5 Next pleat the fabric up to the top ring, keeping the same number of pleats between ribs (struts). They will be slightly smaller at the top on a graduated, i.e sloping, frame. Make sure the pleats are on the straight of

the grain and are pulled up tight both inside and out. If this is not achieved the pleats will not lie well. Whipstitch (oversew) each section of pleats with a double thickness of upholstery thread, securing each pleat.

6 Continue pleating around the frame until the width of fabric is finished. To join another width, trim off the last pleat, turn in the whipped edge on the new piece and start pleating over the last one. To finish off pleating around the frame, tuck the last pleat under the first pleat.

7 When all the pleats are stitched, trim off excess fabric from the top and bottom.

8 Glue or sew on the trim to the top and bottom rings, covering all the stitches and finishing the ends by turning under ¼ in (6 mm).

B O X   P L E A T I N G

raw edge, pin and measure the first pleat, and then fold the fabric back under the pleat to meet the raw edges. Pin this pleat, leave the calculated space between pleats, and begin another pleat.

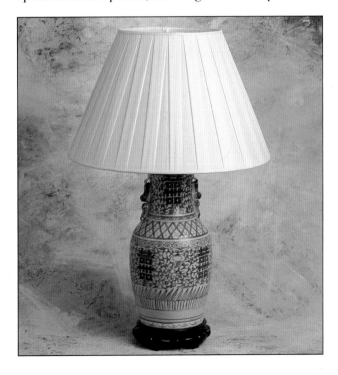

These pleats are the same size at the top as they are at the bottom, and it is only the spacing between the pleats which alters according to the graduation of the frame. Work out the size of the pleat, and the number per gap.

The length of fabric will be three times the circumference of the base and as wide as the depth of a rib (strut) plus 1½ in (4 cm) allowance top and bottom. Cut out as for knife pleating and whip (oversew) the raw edges. Working left to right, start at the bottom rib (strut), turn under the

CANDLE SHADES

*C*andle shades are ideal for wall lights and chandeliers. They can also look effective on tall candlestick bases in the center of a table. The plain straight empire shade in a rich Thai silk would be most fitting for the wall lights around a dining room. There are many unusual and interesting shapes of candle shades. However, a particularly elegant shape is a round bowed

empire swathed in silk chiffon or georgette, and edged in narrow gilt braid or with a pretty butterfly trim made from matching ribbon. Swathing helps to accentuate the bowed frame. Candle shades have an external lining outside the ribs (struts) so that it does not burn with the heat from the bulb. This also gives a firm base to swathe on.

Materials

round bowed empire frame,
butterfly clip
cover fabric, silk chiffon or
similar fabric
lining, silk, crêpe de Chine
narrow gilt braid
pattern paper

½ in (12 mm) lampshade binding
tape
glass-headed pins
upholstery thread
soft pencil
fabric adhesive

---

1 To calculate the amount of fabric required, allow three and a half times the circumference of the base by the diagonal height across two gaps plus 1½ in (4 cm) allowance top and bottom. Cut out the widths of fabric, again as for the pleated shade on the straight of grain, pencil-marking a pleat line 1½ in (4 cm) down from the top. Remove all selvages, and overcast (oversew) the raw edges to prevent fraying.

2 Calculate the number of pleats for the frame as for knife pleating (see page 124).

3 Prepare and bind the frame as on page 120.

4 The lining should be prepared in exactly the same way as for the empire cover (see page 122) with a paper pattern and cut on the bias. Pin and sew the lining onto the outside of the frame, with the seams on the outside. They will later be hidden by the swathing. Do not trim off excess fabric from top and bottom.

5 Prepare and mark the fabric as for the pleated shade. Start pleating at a rib (strut) on the bottom ring, working from left to right. Pleat and pin until one section has been completed.

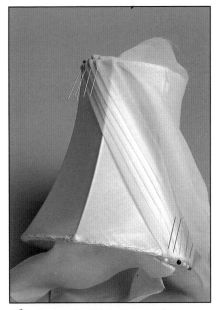

6 To swathe fabric across the top ring, begin draping the pleats up to the second rib (strut) on the left, always maintaining the straight of grain

and the correct number of pleats per gap. This means that the pleats are facing downwards and will not collect too much dust. Make sure all pleats are tight and whipstitch (oversew), securing all pleats.

7 Carry on pleating the whole way around, joining new strips, and finishing as for knife pleating as described on page 125.

8 Trim off excess cover fabric from the top and bottom as close to the stitching as possible. Pull the lining back over the top of the pleats, and oversew on the outside of the rings with upholstery thread. This finishes the top and bottom when a balloon lining is not being inserted.

9 Glue braid around top and bottom to finish.

BUTTERFLY TRIM

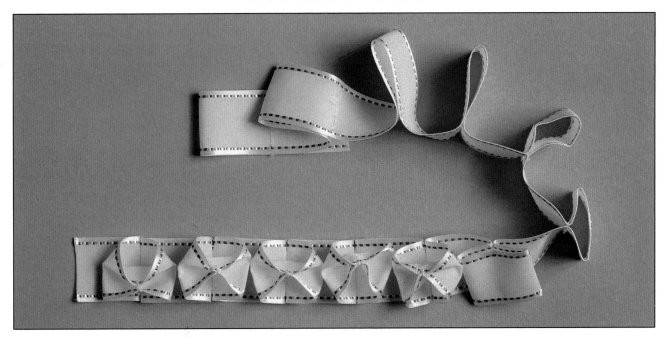

A ribbon butterfly trim is made from box pleats ½ in (12 mm) wide. Allow three times the circumference of the top and bottom ring. Machine sew a pleat 1¼ in (3 cm) wide (therefore using 2½ in (6 cm) of fabric), leave a space of 1¼ in (3 cm), and machine another pleat. Continue until you have enough for the top and

bottom rings. Press these pleats open; they should lie next to one another with no space between. Finally, pinch the top and bottom of the box pleat together and stitch to secure. This gives the butterfly effect.

Butterfly trim can also look attractive on plain or straight pleated shades.

CREATING A STYLE

CREATING A STYLE

*I*n the large houses that serve as a monument to the past, conservators strive to restore or reproduce every period detail as accurately as possible. For most of us the great pleasure of working with a period property is to seek inspiration from that period without following it slavishly. This can result in some fresh and original curtain treatments, which, while they are still sympathetic to the architecture and feel of the building, are not too extreme and expensive.

Curtains were not used before the fifteenth century. At that time windows were usually small and narrow for defensive purposes, and were sometimes covered with oiled waxed paper, not fabric, as this would have reduced the light. After this time, window dressing gradually evolved.

Furniture was also fairly basic with the most comfortable chair reserved for the head of the household. Women and those of lesser social status had to be content with hard seats, perhaps covered by a loose cushion.

While a particular period in history gave rise to different styles in soft furnishings, the most successful interiors combine styles. So the country look can be seen as an amalgam of English cottage and American colonial – simple patterns, comfort, unsophisticated good taste – many of the aspects that evolved from centuries of rural living.

BACK TO THE MIDDLE AGES

The early curtains were mainly found in the grand houses to keep out the sunlight. There was no fixed upholstery, just cushions to soften the hard furniture. There was plenty of fabric, however. Walls were often hung with tapestries. Rich fabrics in narrow widths were seamed together to fit a particular room, often with borders and seams covered with silk or metal lace. Bedhangings were sometimes made of tapestry too. These, like the window curtains, were hung from a pole on rings and pulled to one side when not needed.

To Create the Look

If you are lucky enough to own a home dating from the Middle Ages or you want to recreate that time, the best solution is to keep curtain treatments simple using pairs of curtains or a single curtain hung from a wooden pole or metal rod. If you are able to find some old faded silk or velvet curtains in a shop specializing in antique fabrics, these would look wonderful. A printed fabric with a flamestitch pattern or a fabric with embroidery or crewel work would be sympathetic to the period. The only trimming that is really suitable is braid. Beds, however, were considered very important and these hangings could be trimmed with braid borders and fringes, and a matching bedcover.

EARLY FRENCH STYLE

In the 1680s many French craftsmen fled religious persecution in their own country, thus introducing elsewhere the fashionable styles of the "Sun King's" French Court, particularly with the introduction of *passementerie* – the use of braids and tassels. Fabrics were stretched on walls on specially made wooden frames, and bed and window treatments became more elaborate with generous fringing and the use of tiebacks. Paired curtains were established with valances (pelmets) to hide the rods and rings. Pull-up curtains were another innovation. The French influence was particularly evident on beds where canopies were covered in fabric and topped with carving and even plumes of ostrich feathers. Colors were dark and rich – blacks and reds lifted with sparkling trimmings of metal thread. It was fashionable to have the bed drapes, bedcovers, and chair cushions decorated to match.

To Create the Look

Use full-length paired curtains with a pole covered by a valance (pelmet). Beds can be dressed theatrically and generously trimmed with fringe and braid. Suitable fabrics include damask, moiré, and silk or linen-weave with a block-printed design. Plain shuttered windows or even plantation shutters can suit this early French period style.

The richly colored draperies in the room (above left) evoke a medieval feeling. Similarly, the color and pattern of the hall curtains (left) are reminiscent of medieval wall hangings. Dramatically-swagged brown silk gives a baroque style to the bedroom (above right).

EARLY GEORGIAN

In the eighteenth century, windows were treated as part of the whole decorative scheme and lighter fabrics hung on the walls were to be the forerunners of wallpaper. France, Italy, India, and the Far East now exported fabrics, so there was a wider and more sophisticated range to choose from. By now the 12-pane sash window was almost universal. This light elegance demanded complementary curtain forms such as the pull-up curtain, a simple festoon shade (blind) (see page 66) which, when pulled down, hung flat across the window with no gathering. It was usually made of silk and was unlined. Curtains were topped with a cornice (pelmet) board. In most cases this was finished with a trim of braid

or the curtain fabric, but in very grand houses these boards could be carved and gilded. Colors were sharp and brilliant: blues, candy pinks, and acid greens.

To Create the Look
Keep any curtain treatment simple – this is the key to this period because any frills or flounces immediately produce a more nineteenth-century feel. Variations on the pull-up curtain, plain shutters, or simple pairs of curtains under the valance (pelmet) suit the style. Embroidered or bordered fabrics and strong-colored silks can be used. An authentic window treatment is to place Venetian blinds or roller shades (see page 72) under a valance (pelmet) in order to protect furniture from the sun.

FRENCH ROCOCO STYLE

In the mid 1700s interiors took on a great charm, influenced by delightful French rococo style. Pretty printed cotton textiles gave a much lighter effect, and cherubs and garlands abounded. The fabric used on the walls often matched the window fabric.

To Create the Look

Use Toile de Jouy (traditional designs incorporated hunting and other scenes) or pretty flowered chintzes, festooned or ballooned. In very formal rooms, swags and tails in jewel-colored silks are in keeping with the style (see page 47). Chinoiserie styles are also appropriate.

The bedroom (left) with its dark green walls, canopied bed and elegant sash window evokes the Georgian era. The traditional designs of the Toile de Jouy fabric and matching wallpaper (above) echo the French rococo style.

NEW CLASSICISM

In the latter part of the 1700s the British architect and designer Robert Adam was at the forefront of a new wave of classicism inspired by the discovery of Pompeii and Herculaneum. A huge range of fabrics was available – silks, damasks, brocatelles, watered or brocaded taffetas, velvet, and voile. There was an exciting new palette of colors which included deep turquoise, crushed raspberry, daffodil yellow, and violet. Cords with pulleys were in common use and draw curtains were made to overlap in the center. The British cabinetmaker, Thomas Chippendale, designed carved wooden cornices (pelmets), a feature of the period.

To Create the Look
Use swags and tails (see page 47) trimmed with a neo-classical motif or surmounted by a classical plaster decoration. Pairs of curtains can be topped with draped festoons or valances (pelmets) (see page 39).

For a more rustic, country house look, inspiration comes from Georgian country houses and cottages, as well as the colonial and Shaker styles in the United States. The mood here is mellow, pure and simple, with matte paintwork, and pale sunny colors. Plain fabrics hung from poles at the windows, and beds covered with quilts or coverlets are appropriate unless you have a grand house, where the bed can be draped and covered in printed or embroidered fabric. Shutters or simple window blinds are suitable.

Pompeian red walls with panels depicting Greek mythological figures, and fabrics patterned with classical motifs, contribute to the period feeling of this dining room. In the sitting room (right), the elegance of the Empire style is echoed in the pale sheer fabrics at the window and the gilded fittings.

EMPIRE AND REGENCY

In France, in the late 1700s, the Empire style emerged, inspired by the newly discovered paintings and sculptures in Rome and Egypt. The slightly later Regency style in England was inspired by ancient Greek motifs. Both these styles resulted in a considerable change in the interiors of the period, and a welcome new simplicity. Pull-ups and festoons were no longer fashionable. Pairs of curtains, often voile, topped with elaborately swathed silk draperies, were fixed permanently in position. In England, "The Repository of Arts" magazine was launched. It contained not only curtain styles, but also had real fabric samples stuck to the pages. This was of great importance in influencing interior design.

The mood was formal and curtains were built up in complex layers. Outer curtains were cleverly pinned back in deep scoops, and there were under-curtains in a light fabric, such as silk or voile, and sometimes shades (blinds) that were bordered and hand-painted. Valances (pelmets) were often topped with carved or molded cornices decoratively painted or gilded. Continuous drapery was used to link two or more windows on a single wall, and curtain poles became a decorative feature in their own right. They were molded and gilded with ornate finials. Animal heads, eagles, laurel wreaths, and rosettes were all popular motifs.

Colors were strong – cherry red, deep pink, saffron yellow, strong blues, and golds. Lavish trimmings were used – rich, ornate tassels, and deep heavy fringes. Fabric designs also carried motifs such as laurel wreaths, swans, fleur-de-lis, and the Napoleonic bee. Bed drapery was much simpler than in earlier periods and was elegantly typified by the French Empire style of placing the bed parallel to the wall with a centrally mounted canopy trailing over the curved ends of the bed. Egyptian, Gothic, and Chinoiserie styles and motifs all found their way into this period.

To Create the Look

The look of elegant sophistication is one of the easiest to evoke successfully. The use of motifs, subtle drapery, Empire beds, and gilded curtain poles immediately conjures up the mood and style. White or pale-colored curtains hung on brass rods or draped and swathed over a pole with perhaps a simple roller shade (blind) beneath create an appropriate solution to go with elegant wood furniture.

THE NINETEENTH CENTURY

This era, often referred to as Victorian, produced a proliferation of styles and revivals. The upholsterer became a general supplier for curtains and slipcovers (loose covers) and could also supply craftsmen to decorate interiors, which resulted in a much more coordinated look. The colors were not so dark and gloomy as is generally supposed. There were some magnificent earthy colors, often outlined in black, imperial purple, indigo, and Prussian blue used with gold. Curtains were generally hung from poles, and swags and tails were used a great deal, especially in drawing rooms where the curtains were often "dress" curtains – designed not to pull – only tied back on rosette-headed pins with net or lace curtains underneath.

Everything was fringed, braided or bobbled. Tables and pianos were covered in heavy cloths. Rooms seemed dark because of the use of so much fabric and sometimes the light was kept out altogether with shades (blinds). These were painted, bordered or self-patterned, trimmed with fringes or borders and nearly always made of canvas.

The lambrequin or cantonnière made an appearance during this era. This was a flat valance (pelmet) with a shaped outline which continued down the side of the window, sometimes as far as the floor. Originally, it was designed to hide the bunches of fabric formed when a pull-up curtain was drawn above the window, but soon it became a treatment in its own right, combined with symmetrical main curtains below, and often an asymmetrical voile one as well, caught back in different tiebacks. Slipcovers (loose covers) were introduced and buttoned upholstery was typical of the period. Heavily patterned and textured wallpapers in main rooms and floral prints in bedrooms were popular and everything was stenciled, gilded, and decorated.

To Create the Look

Thick, opulent curtain poles were an authentic feature of the period. This could be the starting point for your treatment. Wood poles can be painted gold, or grained to look like rosewood or mahogany with any decorative motifs picked out in gold. Holdbacks too can be large and elaborate, perhaps with a decorative rosette in brass or ormolu (gilt bronze). Borders and fringes, even on lampshades, are the right trimmings. For a very traditional look, use a single sheer curtain in lace or voile caught back, or a pair crossing over in the center. Modern roller shades (blinds) in cream give an accurate effect.

For a stronger look, shades (blinds) can be in deep green or red. The cord should be fitted with a wooden acorn, not a plastic one, as this defeats the whole period effect. Strong horizontal stripes made up into a shade (blind) are suitable, as are translucent shades (blinds) with a painted design. For main curtains, velvets, wools, and damasks, printed fabrics such as William Morris designs, Gothic patterns, and flower-patterned cottons are appropriate. Tapestry and needlework used for cushions, chair seats and stools, kilim-covered ottomans, oriental rugs, and casually draped paisley shawls also help to conjure up the Victorian spirit.

These two bedrooms have a traditional Victorian atmosphere. Above, it is
achieved by the lace, and the rich colors and patterns of the fabrics. Opposite,
the chaise longue and the continuous valance over the curtains produce the
period atmosphere.

REACTION AT THE END OF THE CENTURY

At the end of the Victorian era, the confusion of styles and over-use of fabric was stifling, and all symmetry and elegance seemed lost. Mass production had resulted in considerable ugliness and poor design and there were predictable reactions against these trends. The Arts and Crafts movement was the beginning of the modern style. William Morris, A. W. N. Pugin, and Owen Jones were important influences, as were the designs of Louis Sullivan and his employee Frank Lloyd Wright in the United States. Walls were treated in three parts – dado, field, and frieze – and the doors were integrated into the overall scheme, often with decoratively painted panels. Colors were soft – olive green, hyacinth blue, plum red or burgundy, lemon, grape, and old rose. White ivory and pale gray were also used.

The flowing elegance of the Art Nouveau style followed on from this, inspired by growing plant forms. Colors were pale – mauves, pinks, greens, turquoises, blues, and yellows.

To Create the Look

Arts and Crafts window treatments should be utterly simple, a wooden pole and lightweight curtains in pale soft colors. Choose patterned upholstery fabrics, decorated with birds, animals, and flowers.

For an Art Nouveau style, rooms should be light and airy and the window treatment in keeping with this. In a formal setting, swags and tails (see page 47) look right if the proportions of the window and room allow, or for a more formal setting, drape a length of fabric over a pole. Curtains over a door as a draft excluder give a typical look of the period (see page 52).

ART DECO

The name Art Deco was derived from the title of the Paris exhibition of 1925, *Exposition des Arts Décoratifs et Industriels*. This was an international exhibition and craftsmen and designers from many countries contributed to the new modern style. Influences included the designs for the Ballets Russes, Egyptian motifs discovered in the tomb of

Tutankhamen, the art movement Cubism, tribal art from Central and South America, and a general obsession with speed in transport – trains, airplanes, and fast cars. It was a luxurious sleek look using contrasting materials such as wood, chrome, glass, leather, and lacquerware. Walls were usually pale shades of beige or off-white, or light-colored wood and wallpaper borders were popular. Motifs abounded – sunrises, fans, stylized trees, flowers, and all animal forms; deer were particularly in vogue. Art Deco was a favorite of Hollywood movie stars, another potent influence.

To Create the Look

Use curtains hung in simple pairs finished off with a shaped, stiffened valance (pelmet). Try to use patterned fabric with geometric or period motifs in muted pastel tones, beiges and browns, or bright oranges, mauves, or lime greens. Venetian blinds (the wide-slatted variety) or curtains simply draped from a chrome pole, also give an authentic feel.

For the upholstery, animal skin prints, leather, or uncut moquette are appropriate. Remember that clean lines are essential to set off the reflective surfaces of an Art Deco room.

Although swags and tails are not associated with Arts and Crafts the restrained version at the window of the room opposite enhances the furniture and woodwork. The sleek lacquered bed and side tables (above), combined with satin bed quilt and pillowcases and the distinctive 1930s-style uplighters, give a strong Art Deco feel to this room.

COUNTRY STYLE

Whether you want to evoke the style of the pretty country cottage with roses over the door or the grand but essentially comfortable country house, the elements are the same, but with a difference of scale.

Small cottage-style windows would originally have been left uncurtained with external shutters. Window dressing to keep out the cold would be simple, with lengths of fabric hanging from a wooden pole. Bedspreads were usually pure white and lacy. In poorer dwellings, thrift would result in patchwork cushions and quilts, and rag rugs on the floor.

The theme for curtain fabrics was usually small floral prints or sprigs with nothing discordant or brash.

To Create the Look

Everything in the country look goes together without looking deliberately coordinated. On small windows, sill-length informal curtains in floral prints or checks with a soft valance (pelmet), if headroom allows, work well. A Roman shade (blind) would add softness but festoons and Austrians could look fussy, depending on the pattern and weight of the fabric.

If your windows are larger, they can take more elaborate treatment, though fabrics should be kept fresh and informal. Smocked or pinch-pleated headings or curtains hung from a pole, or a pleated and ruffled valance to conceal a standard heading, would look in keeping (see page 39). Where headroom allows, a pretty idea is to use a narrow cornice (pelmet) board, perhaps carved and stenciled, that curves upward away from the window with a softly pleated, deeply fringed, shaped valance underneath. This will not only give the treatment a finished look but will allow the maximum light to enter the room, an important feature of the country style. Folding internal shutters or bamboo shades (blinds) could be an alternative for a simpler, more streamlined look.

Brass headboards are traditional, with patchwork or lace bedspreads which can be backed with a colored fabric to coordinate with the rest of the room. Upholstery should be kept simple and comfortable, with perhaps a fringed and patterned shawl draped over a chair or sofa. Slipcovers (loose covers) in floral chintzes are always a popular choice, although wools, velvets, ticking, and brocade are all possibilities. Above all the country look should have a cozy, informal, homey feel.

A stenciled border sets off the sampler over the bed in the fresh and pretty country-style bedroom (left). For a living room, red ticking makes a warm wall covering and works well on the matching roller shades (blinds). Chintz curtains and sisal flooring enhance the country feel. Country style in the kitchen is achieved with sunny yellow walls and cheerful blue checked fabric for curtains, tablecloth, chair covers and cushions.

FRENCH PROVINCIAL STYLE

The yellow light of the Mediterranean sun heats up colors, so cool colors are important to this vibrant style. The distinctiveness of the Provençal look comes from the natural materials used in the houses of the area – local stones, terra-cotta tiles, or marble for the floor, with rugs. Garden furniture would be wrought iron, cane, or bamboo. Inside are decorative wood chests and cupboards, along with other special decorative accents of the region to give the right atmosphere.

To Create the Look
Color and fabric weight are all-important. Heavy fussy curtains will look out of place. Keep window treatments simple. Try pencil- or French-pleated headings (see page 36), pairs of curtains on poles, or lightweight unlined fabrics softly swagged and draped over a pole. Ticking and small French-Provincial-style printed fabrics with their distinctive traditional prints, like the teardrop, can look pretty for bedroom curtains and tablecloths. Lace is used on door curtains and flat across the window, but choose heavy cotton off-white lace with recognizable motifs that can be centered as a feature.

The bedroom isn't a fussy over-furnished room in this style. A simple cream linen or cotton cover with perhaps a flat valance (pelmet) at the window would evoke peaceful simplicity.

MODERN STYLE

This century has seen many different approaches to style including classical modern, "International Moderne," Bauhaus and high-tech. Interiors have become more streamlined, clean, and uncluttered with a mix of matte and reflective materials. Lighting is of great importance and all the items are chosen with great care.

Everything has its place and cleverly designed storage accommodates the electrical appliances – television and stereo. Well-placed shelving displays dramatic collections. The scheme may even center around one special piece of furniture such as a leather chair. Colors are paler and cooler and the windows are integrated into the scheme like everything else in the room.

To Create the Look
To achieve a truly modern look, you have to be disciplined – especially if you are seeking the minimalist approach, in which case the only textiles used might be the cushions on a leather sofa or the window treatment. Windows need to be unobtrusive with Roman shades (blinds), Venetian or micro blinds, transparent silk festoons, or unlined fabric in a neutral color.

Another approach to the modern look that incorporates the exotic is a clean Japanese style with a futon, sliding screens, wooden floors, and carefully chosen plants and accessories.

Red and green Souleiado fabrics (left) are inherently French provincial. Modern interiors can be dramatic, as in the striking blue-and-turquoise color scheme (below right), or pleasingly simple with tiled floor, pine chest and natural-colored shades (blinds) (top right).

CREATING A MOOD

If you are not really interested in a particular style but prefer to plan your room around a mood, then think of an adjective such as romantic or sunny and work from there. There is plenty of scope for the romantic, a look that is soft and pretty.

Symmetrically or asymmetrically draped sheers, carefully trimmed with silk ribbon or ball (bobble) fringes look ravishingly pretty. If blocking out of light is required, a simple roller shade (blind) underneath does the trick. Deep ruffles (frills) or knife-edge pleats and lavish curtains cascading on the ground convey the mood perfectly. Festoons and Austrians (see pages 64 to 66) in the right colors and fabrics also look very romantic, with cleverly placed rosettes or bows outlined in a contrasting color.

Beds can be dressed to look romantic – the possibilities are endless (see page 90). Lace bedcovers, crisp white linen, ruffled dressing table skirts, are all part of the romantic look.

The exotic look can be created with color and clever accessorizing. Rich "spicy" colors – gold, cinnamon, peach, spiked with acid yellow – collections of jars, oriental vases, patterned rugs, oriental motifs, Chinese wallpapers, and fretwork, would all evoke this comfortable style. For the windows, louvered shutters, simple roller shades (blinds), voile on metal rods, or elegantly simple Italian strung curtains are possible solutions (see page 37).

For a sunny feeling in a room, paint the walls yellow to reflect the light. Blue and yellow make a traditional and charming combination and the blue prevents the yellow from being too overpowering in a room where sun shines in most of the day.

Any scheme that "brings the garden inside" with perhaps cane furniture, trellis wallpaper, and plants brings a sunny mood.

*Pink walls, bows on the occasional table, and tulips create a romantic corner
(left), whereas the array of vibrant checks and stripes (above), and the heavily-
gilded furniture and rich red-and-gold fabric (top) lend
exotic moods to these interiors.*

Yellow curtains edged with a ruffle (frill), are left unlined and tied back to let the sunshine in.

A sunny mood in the room above is achieved through a clever combination of pastel fabrics for the cushions covering the wicker furniture. Subtle pastels are also the choice for chair covers and matching curtains (top) to make the most of this light-and-bright room.

FEATURE IDEAS

CURTAIN TREATMENT

Problem Windows

A carefully chosen and thought-out curtain treatment can work a special magic in an interior. Not only can it set the style and mood of the room, but it can overcome structural inadequacies and create the illusion of more, or less, space by the strategic placing of a rod or track or pole, the use of color and pattern, and the shape of the treatment you choose.

Before deciding on a particular treatment, consider the following checklist:

- the function of the room
- the shape of the window
- the view beyond
- the amount of wall space and headroom available
- the architectural style of the room
- particular features in that room (such as a heavy fireplace)
- the look/style/mood you want to create in the room.

FRENCH DOORS (WINDOWS)

These are fairly straightforward unless they are inward opening. If this is the case, and headroom and wall space allow, extend the pole or rod or track well beyond the ends of the frame, so that the doors can open unimpeded. A traditional way of treating French doors (windows) is to use panels of sheer fabric or lace attached to the top and bottom of the frame by wire rods (see page 52), with dress curtains (these are curtains that do not pull across the window) on either side as in illustration A.

If blocking out light is not a priority, then you might consider a draped valance (pelmet), perhaps an attractive swag over a pole. The Victorians often used highly decorative shawls for this purpose (illustration B).

Simple shades (blinds) – roller or Roman – are a good idea where space is limited or where the French door or window is recessed.

A

B

C

ARCHED WINDOWS

Where space permits use a pole or traverse rod
(track) set well above the arch for a pair of
curtains or a single curtain. Alternatively, festoon
or Austrian shades (blinds) as in illustration D
(see pages 64 to 66), or draperies with a fixed
heading on a curved fixture (illustration C) look in
keeping with the window shape. These are closed
either by releasing them from tiebacks and
allowing the curtains to drop down, or with
"Italian stringing." This works on the same
principle as festoon and Austrian shades (blinds)
with strings through rings, except that they are
strung on a curved trajectory so that the curtains
pull up to the side.

In a more modern setting, fine-slatted Venetian
blinds with curtains as an outer frame work well,
or you might favor the eighteenth-century British
critic and man of letters Horace Walpole's purist

D

approach. He was reputed to have said, "Allow the shape of the window to speak for itself with no distraction from blinds or curtains."

SKYLIGHTS

Sheer fabric anchored on rods or wires at the top and bottom of the sloping window diffuse the light. If blocking out of light is required, use a Venetian blind, fixing either end of the frame, or some sort of fabric shade (blind)—Roman or roller—held by strategically placed rods.

Some rooflights can be fitted with shades or blinds between two layers of glass to make a neat double-glazed unit. The shade or blind is controlled from below.

DORMERS

A dormer is a window projecting from an attic room or loft where there is a sloping ceiling. The most usual method of fixing curtains is with a rod (track) or pole within the side walls of the dormer, close against the window (illustration E).

If space is too restricted, one solution is to slot curtains on one or a pair of hinged rods, so that they can be swiveled open to rest against the

dormer wall during the day. Sheers can be used behind the main curtains, threaded onto narrow wires or rods at the top and bottom of the window itself. If there is sufficient headroom and wall space, use a pole or rod (track) outside the frame, with lightweight curtains held back by tiebacks, as shown in illustration F.

F

SMALL WINDOWS

If the house has more than two floors, the upper windows may be smaller and so the window treatment should be adapted. Choose fabrics that are lighter in weight, plain, or with small-scale patterns, and reduce the proportions of the treatment accordingly. For example, headings can be used but should not be too deep.

Sill-length curtains are preferable on small windows, ideally stopping just a little below the sill which will make it seem deeper.

If privacy or blocking out of light are not of prime importance, as in a hall or a landing, then consider making a feature of a small window in other ways by perhaps painting or stenciling a border around the frame (wallpaper borders could also be used). This makes the window seem larger. The frame of the window itself can also be given an interesting paint treatment.

E

WINDOWS SET CLOSE TOGETHER

Make any windows that are close together seem like a deliberate pair by using two pairs of curtains, hung on one pole or rod (track).

— TALL, NARROW WINDOWS —

Do not overdress tall windows. You may spoil the architectural detail. Traditionally the hallmark of colonial, federal and Georgian architecture, these windows usually have fine frames. A simple festoon (see page 66) set within the frame, or over it (illustration G), or a flat Roman shade (blind) (see page 68), will show the frame off well (illustration I). A single curtain caught diagonally across the frame can be effective (illustration H), or try draperies in a plain fabric with a simple swag draped over a pole above. Avoid top-heavy valance treatments, and be generous with the curtains as this will make the window seem wider.

H

G

I

WIDE WINDOWS

It is not easy to curtain wide windows successfully; they often seem overdressed, rather like a stage set. They can also be a serious source of drafts, so extend the traverse rod (track) or pole well beyond the sides of the frame, wherever wallspace allows, to cut out drafts. Unless there is a windowsill to break their fall, the curtains should always be floor length, lined, and preferably interlined, for insulation.

If the curtains meet in the middle of the window on the rod, track or pole, and are then caught or tied back, it will give the effect of reducing the width of the window. Similarly, a softly shaped valance, perhaps pleated or smocked, will reduce the impact of over-large windows.

Diffuse an unattractive view or harsh light with sheers. Keep fabric subdued, plain or textured, but if you decide to use a pattern, choose something bold and clear, such as broad vertical stripes. If you wish to use shades (blinds), Roman or roller, choose a plain fabric with a contrasting border for interest and definition. It is better to avoid Austrians or festoons which will look fussy and cluttered.

J

BAY WINDOWS

These days there are special rods (tracks) and brackets available for bay windows. Where the window frames are light and the windows close together, consider using a single pair of curtains on each side of the bay (illustration K); but with heavier frames, and more space between the windows, intermediate curtains between them work well (illustration J). A wide bay can also take individual Austrians or festoons as in illustration L.

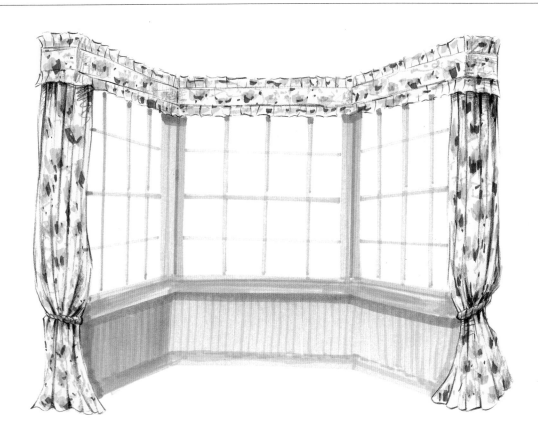

K

L

SHUTTERED WINDOWS

Shutters are an excellent barrier against noise, weather, and crime. New shutters can be made by a good carpenter or, alternatively, louvered and plantation shutters can be bought from builders' suppliers or specialty retailers.

For working shutters you might decide to do without curtains altogether, and give the shutters an interesting paint or stain treatment on both sides. If you are going to use curtains, then have the pole or rod or track well extended beyond the window, to give the shutter complete freedom of movement.

For fixed shutters, Roman or roller shades (blinds) look good within the recess of the window. Or consider a festoon hung over the frame. For curtains, use a pole or rod or track that is well extended, so that the shutters can still be seen during the day (illustration M).

SIDE-SWINGING DOOR OR WINDOW

For a casement window or glass-panel door, use a shade, blind or café curtains fixed onto a frame, so that they open when the door or window opens, see illustration N.

WINDOWS SET AT ANGLES

Where two windows are at right angles to each other, place a pair of curtains with one at each side of the two windows. Put two more curtains where the two windows meet, and tie these, one at each side, so they meet in the middle as a pair when drawn during the day, as shown in illustration O.

WINDOW IN A TIGHT CORNER

For a window that is wedged into a corner, no window treatment may be necessary. If something is required, then use a shade, blind, or a single curtain.

M

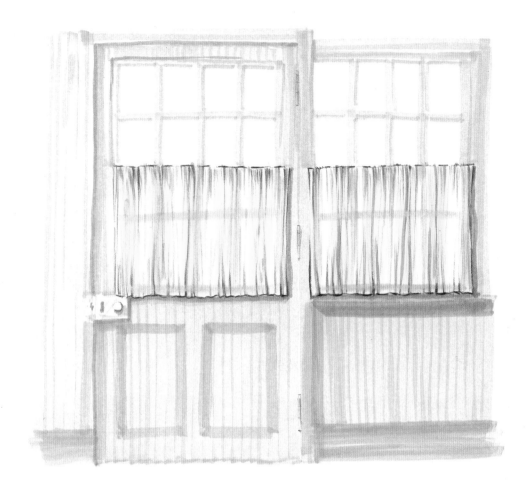

N

O

P

DOOR AND WINDOW TOGETHER

Where the door and window are adjacent, put a pole or rod or track straight across the top of both. Place a pair of curtains with one at each end of the door and window, and a third curtain in between the two (illustration P). Or use dress curtains at either end of the door/window combination and fix shades or blinds over the panes on the door/window.

USE OF COLOR

*D*ark colors absorb light and shapes and intensify the surrounding colors. Light colors, on the other hand, reflect light and absorb the surrounding colors, making rooms look larger and ceilings higher.

Neutrals such as gray and beige make a good general background, and work well with objects, pictures, and contrasting colors.

Your choice of color will be vital to the mood of the room. Is it to be warm and inviting or cool and elegant? Colors will dictate this. Less sunny rooms will have a cold and quite harsh light which colors, such as reds, oranges, and yellows will counteract to create a warm comfortable mood. In very sunny rooms, you might decide to cool these down with the use of greens, blues, or purples.

Texture also affects the value of color. A matte, rough fabric will absorb light, and a shiny fabric will reflect it. Therefore a shiny fabric can help create a feeling of more space.

USE OF PATTERN

*T*oo many patterns can make a room seem cluttered. If you decide to use more than one printed fabric in a room, your choices must be carefully coordinated. Pattern in window dressing should be used in proportion to the size of the window where it will be used. So choose small prints in small rooms and on small windows, and larger designs in large rooms and on large windows. To use a large pattern repeat on a small window would create an imbalance in the scheme.

Where windows and surrounding walls or ceilings are awkwardly shaped, the impact can be reduced by using the same pattern on the walls and windows. To draw attention to the window, choose strong colors and strong patterns.

POSITIONING OF ROD, TRACK, OR POLE

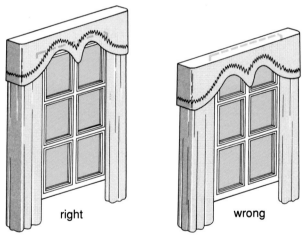

right   wrong

To give an illusion of height, place the rod, track, or pole well above the window. For a very wide window, consider hanging the curtains inside the frame to hide part of the window. To increase the amount of light coming into the room, extend the rod, track, or pole well past the window so that the curtains can be drawn back.

Remember that the most intense light enters a room from ceiling height, so in low-ceilinged rooms avoid valances (pelmets) and use a decorative heading on the curtains instead.

To DISGUISE WINDOWS

If you have a window that is metal-framed or of unpleasant proportions, use a draped style to soften any hard lines. Choose colors and patterns that blend well with the rest of the room, making the window look less dominant. Lead the eye away from architectural deficiencies with carefully placed trimmings such as rosettes or choux (see page 43) with contrasting piping.

To disguise an unattractive view, consider using roller shades or blinds underneath the curtains. These could be in a contrasting color, a contrasting pattern, or even have a design painted on them. There is a wide range of sheers available nowadays in many colors and these can successfully diffuse a harsh light or ugly view.

To ENLARGE A SMALL ROOM

To make a small room seem larger, use pale colors and small-scale patterns that harmonize with the rest of the scheme. Avoid over-elaborate treatment and low-hanging valances (pelmets) as these will block out light. Keep your treatment light and balanced.

To BRIGHTEN A DARK ROOM

Light, warm-toned colors will reflect light and give a welcoming feel to a dingy room. However, if the room is mainly used at night, which is often the case with a dining room, you might decide to exploit the darkness of the room with a rich dark color scheme, and use dramatic pools of light to add interest.

SHOWHOUSE REVIEW

A welcoming landing (opposite) is decorated in warm colors and has a bold border that enhances the display of prints. Above, a cushion-filled window seat makes a cozy retreat in the wide hallway.

HALLS, LANDINGS, AND STAIRS

*H*alls are often narrow passages and they need careful thought in the choice of color and lighting. To maximize the feeling of space, carry the decorative scheme up the stairs as well. Choose practical, hard-wearing finishes throughout the hall, landing, and stairs. These areas suffer the most wear and tear, especially in a family home. Your hall is also important because it gives the first impression of your home and should, therefore, be warm and welcoming.

In a front hall, if there are drafts from the front door, a curtain on a pole (a portière) is a good way of excluding them. Sometimes a curtain can be used as a barrier between the hall and the rest of

the house. A landing with a window at the top of the stairs lends itself to an interesting treatment; the window can be a focal point. However, if the window and landing have particularly interesting architectural features, you might decide on a simpler treatment or leave them completely plain. Stained glass and decorative glass panels can be effective in a hall, and are best left as a feature in their own right with no surrounding fuss.

From a safety point of view it is important not to restrict light on stairs. Unless you are dealing with very large spaces, choose fabric that blends with the walls. A contrast will break up the space and make it seem smaller.

*Sunlight glows through the yellow Roman blinds, and pine furniture reinforces
the country style of the kitchen opposite. Above, the plant-filled kitchen is light
and airy, enhanced by the ribbon-patterned fabric used for
the shade (blind) and the curtains.*

KITCHENS

*T*he kitchen is mainly a functional room, so safety and hygiene must be a top priority. Grease and cooking smells tend to cling to fabrics and textured shades (blinds), so washable fabrics in a clean, unfussy style are the best choice. Roller shades (blinds) can be treated to give a wipeable surface. They can be plain or patterned, have a design painted on them, and can be trimmed in a variety of ways.

Roman shades (blinds) in a light fabric give a slightly softer look. If using pairs of curtains, keep them short for safety and position them well away from the stove (hob). Consider having them unlined or with a detachable lining so that washing is not a problem. Where the eating area is separate from the functional part of the kitchen, there is more scope for window treatments and you could choose something a little more elaborate to harmonize with the simpler treatments in the cooking area.

*The elegance of the room (above), with its floor-length curtains surmounted by
gathered valances at the tall windows, contrasts with the simplicity of the
dining area opposite, where striped slip covers provide the only softening touch.*

DINING ROOMS

*B*efore deciding on a treatment for your dining room, consider whether the room will be used frequently or on special occasions only. In the latter case, you could indulge in a lavish treatment.

Consider too, if the room will be used mainly at night or if it will also be used regularly in the daytime.

For night drama, choose rich colors, highlighted with carefully placed pools of light. For all-around use, try a fresher scheme with sunny color on printed fabrics. For a more modern look, Venetian, Roman or micro blinds in colors to match the rest of the scheme look smart and up-to-date.

These days, a separate dining room is quite a luxury. Sunroom extensions are a popular choice for extra dining space, but often one end of a living room or a large kitchen is used. This can work successfully, particularly with good lighting and perhaps a decorative screen to hide the debris at the end of a meal. An old table can be transformed with a pretty cloth, candles, fresh flowers, and crystal.

*Comfort can enhance workrooms. The library (above) is aglow with mahogany
bookshelves, whose fine detailing complements the leather-bound books. Full
curtains and a cushion-filled sofa invite relaxation. The traditional study
(opposite) has warm apricot walls and rich green curtains hung from poles,
caught back at either side of the dormer window, making a luxurious treatment
for an unusually contoured wall.*

LIBRARIES, STUDIES AND WORKROOMS

Whether you want a relaxed traditional look or something more brisk and efficient, the working light will be important, so avoid low-hanging swags and valances because the strongest light enters the room at the top of the window. Thin-slatted Venetian blinds look good in a more modern setting, while simple curtains in a warm, rich fabric are effective for a mellow look. If the room is to be used at night, use warm colors and thick-textured fabrics for coziness. If the light is too strong, use a transparent roller shade (blind) or a Venetian blind to filter the light.

*Swags and tails create an elegant look (top), while the draperies
in the room above have a country style. The sitting room
opposite doubles as a guest room; during the day the bed is
disguised with a striped cover, bolsters and cushions.*

SITTING ROOMS

*T*raditionally these rooms have the most lavish treatments in the house. In high-ceilinged, well-proportioned rooms, swags and tails can look wonderful, but avoid them in low, ill-proportioned rooms as they would only exaggerate the problem. If you prefer something simple, consider plain curtains with a shaped stiffened valance (pelmet) bound with a contrasting border for definition.

Floor-length draperies tied back with fabric, cords, or clips, with valances (pelmets) or swags and trim, work best in these rooms. The choice of fabrics includes damask, velvet, heavy silk or cotton, plain and printed linen, heavy jacquard weave, chenille, chintz, or wool. Plains, stripes, checks, florals, and self-patterned fabric all work well. You might decide on a scheme with strong rich colors or, alternatively, a subtle monochrome scheme. Trimmings are all important. Contrasting edges or borders, colored lining brought around to the front, tassels, and fringes can all be effective.

In some houses, particularly Victorian ones, there is a gap (usually called a deadlight) between the top of the window architrave and the ceiling or cornice. If the height of the ceiling dictates that a valance (pelmet) is necessary, attach this to the curtain rod (track) or pole. It will look soft and pretty when curtains are drawn back during the day, and resemble a full treatment at night.

Remember that whatever you choose for the window draperies should harmonize with the furniture in the room so that, for example, where there is heavy furniture, this is balanced with a rich heavy fabric.

*Sprigged chintz, ferns and a wicker basket give the bathroom above a country
atmosphere. Sheer curtains in a bathroom provide both privacy and light, as in
both rooms opposite. In the upper photograph, a comfortable chair and a
generous display of cushions add soft touches to an otherwise
purely functional room.*

BATHROOMS

*T*he best fabric for bathrooms is cotton, as wool retains moisture, and silk tears easily if wet. Privacy is one important consideration, and draft exclusion may be another. You will also need something that is part of the whole decorative scheme to soften the hard and shiny surface of the tiles and fixtures.

Shades or blinds work well (see pages 60 to 75), or try Roman, roller (perhaps framed by a lambrequin, see page 39), Venetian, wood and cane, festoon, Austrian, or even slatted shutters. If there is sufficient space, hang curtains as well; this is particularly welcoming in a country bathroom. Lace panels, voile, cheesecloth, net and muslin, sheer or lacy fabrics for festoons, or Austrians and internal shutters are all possibilities in the bathroom.

SUNROOMS

Lloyd Loom chairs and flowered chintz cushions create a charming period atmosphere.

Sunrooms with their expanses of glass are prey to extremes of heat and cold. Window coverings are essential to protect both people and plants. Many companies specialize in shades or blinds for sunrooms so there is a huge choice available. Wooden blinds and cotton shades are among the most usual. Shades or blinds in a dark color will deflect the light.

As an attractive alternative, loosely drape a light fabric from the ceiling so it billows. The fabric must be closely woven if it is to shield you from the light and be fade resistant. Sheeting is a good choice. Always use materials that are resistant to fungicides in a sunroom.

B E D R O O M S

This sunny bedroom has bold blue walls that are echoed in the bright bed cover.

*B*edrooms are private and peaceful rooms, somewhere to retreat from the hurly-burly of the rest of the house. They can be pale and romantic or dark and mysterious. It is important to control the light in bedrooms. If the window faces the rising sun it might be wise to use a light-excluding fabric, or add Venetian blinds. (These are available in a wide range of attractive colors that will harmonize with your decorative scheme.)

Curtains have a light look if used in conjunction with shades or blinds. Sheers look interesting combined with heavier outer curtains. If you want your bedroom to be bright and airy, avoid fabrics that are too somber and heavy. Cotton, silk, chintz, and brocade fabrics all work well.

Choose the headboard carefully with comfort in mind. You can cover headboards in fabric to go with the decorative scheme (see page 98), or try a wooden-framed headboard with a padded center for comfort. Brass headboards are decorative but you will need plenty of comfortable cushions.

Shaped valances on the four-poster bed and the windows give softness to this country-style bedroom (top), while the color scheme of light and dark blue and white makes a cool haven of the room above. The colors are echoed in the patchwork that provides a striking focal point above the bed.

NURSERIES

A riot of French provincial prints creates a vibrant and original nursery.

Choose an adaptable scheme that will grow with your child. Children like bold colors; but avoid a scheme that is so strong and stimulating that it discourages sleep! Keep the window treatment simple; try a plain fabric, for example, trimmed with a simple border to bring in more color and pattern.

Curtains can be hung beneath a cornice (pelmet) board painted in a contrasting color or with a pattern stenciled on it; a Roman shade (blind) or a roller shade (blind) can be combined with a pair of short, unlined curtains. Consider using light-resistant roller shades (blinds) or adding a blackout lining to curtains to encourage sleep.

Be aware of safety in nurseries. Put in good safe lighting and make certain there is nothing harmful within reach of the baby or toddler.

CHILDREN'S AND TEENAGERS' BEDROOMS

Go for a simple style that can be easily and inexpensively adapted and updated as the child grows up. Choose a practical, stylish scheme that will take the inevitable knocks. Children often use their rooms like a playroom so the beds should be dressed accordingly to withstand being lain on and sat on regularly. Plenty of storage will be needed and it is a good idea to incorporate this into your scheme at the beginning. If you decide on a particularly pretty scheme, avoid long drapes or trailing bedcovers that could easily be stepped on or damaged. Ruffles (frills), borders, tiebacks, and ribbons achieve the effect more economically.

For a bold scheme you might consider using primary colors or a soft neutral scheme that would be an ideal background for the inevitable posters and colorful clutter that gather over the years. Shades and blinds in all forms are a practical choice for these rooms and lambrequins or wooden cornice (pelmet) boards painted with an appropriate design can smarten up the room.

Two complementary fabric designs have been skillfully combined in the child's room above. The bed quilt is in the same fabric as the curtains, and both the curtain valance and the bed dust ruffle (valance) match each other, with the duck motif cleverly continued in the wall frieze. The room opposite is a delightful place for a teenage girl. The canopied bed, festoon shade (blind) with smocked heading, and the quilted bed cover all contribute to the pretty, feminine style.

THE
WORKROOM

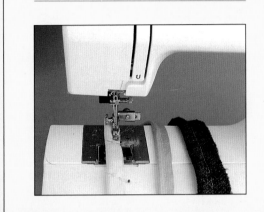

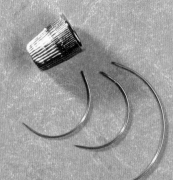

THE START

Soft furnishings can play a major part in determining the color scheme of a room. These bedspreads, draperies, cushions, and footstools have been carefully planned so that although each is in cream and blue colors, together they display a cleverly coordinated variety of patterns and designs.

Decorating a new house or a new room can be a daunting task. You are bound to be faced with the frightening thought "Where do I start?" "Do I choose the wallpaper or the carpet first?" The answer is to look at your existing furniture and lifestyle. All rooms are basically white boxes. Our aim should be to put our individual stamp into the white box; to put a little of our own personality there; to make the building or room come alive in a manner that we find comfortable, attractive, and easy to live in.

The twentieth century has been a time of intensive decoration, restoration, and preservation of period houses, as well as the redevelopment and construction of contemporary buildings. The choice of decoration in new houses should be partially influenced by the period of the house. Generally, bold geometric prints do not suit a

house that is 300 years old with beams in the ceilings and walls and small leaded windows, just as a small print will be lost in an enormous sitting room with very high ceilings. However, there are no set rules and some bold designers rip out all the period features in a house and fabricate a style of their own. Often this is amusing and decorative and, when well done, quite an achievement.

In a situation where a whole room is going to be redecorated, the first decision is the type of colors that are preferred. Do you feel like a change this time? Have a good discussion with friends and family about your intentions and the feedback will often form the basis of something successful. Look out the window at the view beyond. If in a country environment, it is best not to choose a fabric that will clash with nature; if overlooking a townscape, something brighter would be more appropriate. If the room is in a sunny position, you might want to use a cool, neutral scheme, or hot, vibrant colors in a dingy situation.

If you are doing up a bedroom, will you need sheer curtains or a similar fine voile or sheer fabric for the sake of privacy? Obviously this will mean that the view is not of prime importance.

Most of us have the odd chair or rug or piece of furniture that we can't give up. It is often of sentimental value rather than perhaps great commercial value or beauty. If this is the case, some form of color scheme and layout will have to be arranged so as to enhance and blend with this furniture or textile. The subtle balance of old and new in a newly decorated property is often the reason why a house feels welcoming. Frequently all that is needed to change the appearance of that well-traveled set of armchairs is a lot of brightly colored cushions harmonizing with the new color scheme. Similarly, a different colored tablecloth or throw will add something new at minimal cost.

THE WORKROOM

In order to make the task ahead successful and as much fun as possible, it is worth the time and effort involved to prepare yourself for the job in hand. Not everyone is fortunate enough to have the space at home to put aside a complete room for making soft furnishings, but make some arrangements, so that you will not be disturbed too often. A large work surface is essential. The floor or a long table is the obvious answer when making curtains. If you are using a table, it should be high enough so as not to give you a backache. It is worth putting blocks under the legs to raise it, so that you do not have to bend at all. Make sure the table is clean, and, if wooden, that it is free from any sticky polish or dust. Laminates are not always easy to sew on, so if possible, cover the table with a cloth. Secure it underneath the table, so that it will not slip. The task will be much quicker if all the equipment is at hand, and you can move around easily. If possible, position your work in natural light, otherwise place individual lamps in such a way as to avoid shadows falling over the work. The best and least tiring lighting is a fluorescent tube.

ESSENTIAL SEWING EQUIPMENT

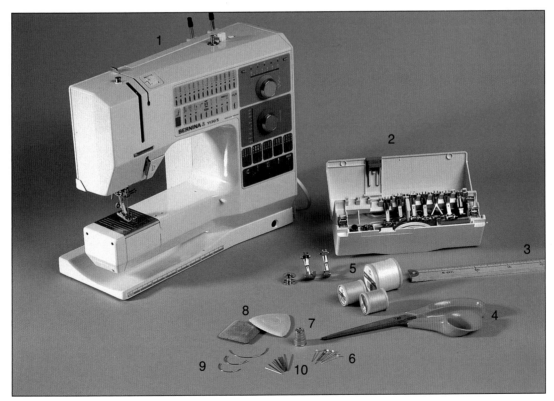

1 sewing machine	5 threads	9 curved upholstery needles
2 attachments	6 glass-headed pins	10 various sewing needles
3 yardstick (meter ruler)	7 thimble	
4 long-bladed scissors	8 dressmaker's or tailor's chalks	

THE SEWING MACHINE

Beautiful sewing is the union of thread and fabric, proper needle size, the right tension, and the appropriate stitch size. Often when sewing soft furnishing fabrics, you will find that the bulk of the fabric causes a strain on your domestic machine. Keep it well oiled and baste (tack) fabric layers wherever possible to relieve the strain. You will need a zigzag stitch and a reverse setting for finishing off seams and miters.

ATTACHMENTS

Depending on the work to be done, there are various sewing machine feet available; follow the manufacturer's handbook if you are in doubt. It is a good idea to have several spare bobbins, already wound with different colored threads—one for the main fabric, one for the lining, and one for the trim of the fabric, etc. If these are wound at the beginning of the job it will save time.

A little brush is useful for cleaning the accessible working parts of the machine where particles of dust may be trapped.

MACHINE NEEDLES

Look at the chart for your make of sewing machine for the correct size of needle. If too fine a needle is used, the thread will fray during sewing, and if you are sewing thicker cloth, the needle will break. Too heavy a needle in lightweight cloth causes the seams to split.

PINS

Small steel pins can be bought in large boxes, but large pins with colored glass tops are best for soft furnishing. They do not hurt your finger tips as you push them into the fabric, and they do not get lost or forgotten in the fabric because they are easy to see. They are also longer, which is useful when digging through several layers of fabric, interlining, and lining. Don't use pins on suede and leather, use adhesive tape. This comes in several forms and is useful when doing hems. A pincushion makes it easier to store and work with pins, and a magnet is useful for dropped pins.

SEWING NEEDLES

These should be varied according to the type of fabric that is being sewn. It is not always possible to sew every seam by machine, so a good stock of hand-sewing needles should be kept for various uses. They are classified in three ways—in thickness, length and size, and shape of eye. They fall into several categories:

Betweens: Fairly similar to sharps but smaller and shorter; used for medium and heavyweight fabrics, quilting, and detailed handwork.

Bodkins: Blunt, long-eyed, and thick, used to thread cord, ribbon or elastic through a casing.

Embroidery: A fine needle with a long eye for easier threading. Used for embroidery, crewel work, smocking, and general purpose sewing.

Milliner's-Straw Needles: Larger than sharps and used for basting (tacking) and other stitches where length speeds up the work.

Sharps: A long, oval-eyed needle for most purposes.

Upholstery: Curved needles with large eyes, also used for making lampshades.

Scissors
Make sure you have one large pair of stainless steel shears to cut out thick pieces of fabric. They should be strong, perhaps with a flat blade on one side, fairly heavy, and around 10 in (25 cm) long. It is useful to have a smaller pair just to snip off threads as you sew. These should have a sharp point to unpick seams and areas that are difficult to get at, or to trim a complex shape. Make sure that these scissors are not used for any other purpose, so that they are always very sharp.

STEAMERS AND IRONS

Pressing is all important when sewing; no article will look totally professional if not properly pressed. Turnings and seams should be well pressed for a good finish and care taken to choose the right heat setting. Velvet should not be pressed, only steamed, otherwise the pile will flatten. Take care with silk as it might watermark. A small hand steamer is a good investment because it steams *in situ*. Creases can be taken out of curtains without taking them down, and any fabric will benefit immediately from a short treatment, saving trouble and expense. A steam iron is not always necessary, although a wet cloth should be used when pressing, and care taken that the glaze is not removed from chintz.

TAPE MEASURES

It is worth having a large metal measuring tape that expands to at least 10 ft (3 meters) for curtains, and a smaller soft one to measure around corners and difficult curves. These can be in U.S. Customary or imperial, or in metric measures, depending on what you are used to, but once you have decided, stick to that system, or there will be mistakes. A ruler is very useful, either plastic, metal, or wood, when measuring out a perfect square on flat fabric for cutting out cushions, or when used like a compass for making a circular tablecloth, or circular cushions.

Tailor's or dressmaker's chalk

This is a useful way of marking both light and dark fabrics instead of tailor's tacks. It comes in several forms: flat, pencil shaped with a brush on the end, and now in powder form in a fine-line dispenser.

Thimble

A much forgotten but very useful aid, it is essential when pushing needles through heavy fabrics, and it also protects the fingertips.

THREAD

When choosing thread, you need to consider color and composition. The thread on the spool will appear darker than when it is sewn into the fabric. Although there are many multi-purpose threads on the market, watch out for the correct weight and fiber to match the fabric you intend to sew.

FABRICS

Fabrics fall into several categories and the impact they create depends largely on whether or not they are suitable for that use. As well as color and pattern, you should take into consideration texture, weight, and practicality. Color is usually the first thing to consider. When putting several colors together group them and, if possible, get large samples and stick them up on the wall, so that they can be seen in all lights.

This way you can judge their mood and their impact from a distance. The colors may merge, in which case you should choose something stronger, perhaps in the form of a texture or a pattern. The choices are immediately expanded to include patterns which come in colorful and subtle floral prints, bold geometric and abstracts, small and large checks, bold and subdued stripes, large bouquets and small mini prints – all shapes and

*A selection of pattern types. Left to right, lower layer: subtle floral,
abstract/geometric, subdued stripes, dark-colored traditional oakleaf,
regular geometric with muted jewel colors. Upper layer: chintz in solid
colors, floral with predominantly white background, all-over floral
design in bright colors.*

sizes within the color spectrum. If choosing is
difficult, coordinated patterns are the answer,
although there is much pleasure in mixing colors
and patterns to end up with the perfect blend.

If you decide to choose a pattern, remember
that it will be multiplied many times on curtains,
so choose the size accordingly. High rooms need
larger patterns, whereas mini prints look lost in a
large expanse, especially at a distance where a
bolder fabric, say a geometric or floral pattern,
would be more dramatic. Subtle coloring looks
clever but it may disappear in a large room.
Tastes change, so consider wisely before choosing
a fashionable contemporary print that you may tire
of in a year or two.

When mixing patterns, the combination of
textures is important, so make sure that they
complement and harmonize, so that the fabric is
shown at its best. If you choose a beautiful pattern
that you want to appreciate, make sure that it
appears on a flat surface somewhere, such as on a
slipcover or on curtains.

When buying fabrics for soft furnishings, check
with the salesperson if you are unsure about
whether your choice is suitable for the particular
purpose. Hard work can be wasted if, for
example, a loose-weave fabric used for slipcovers
sags after less than a year. Some dress fabrics can
be used in soft furnishing – a bed cushion, as part
of patchwork, or on special bedcovers, but
generally it is wise to stick with the fabric
appropriate for the purpose. Try not to fall in love
with a color or pattern before you have checked its
suitability.

Always check the fabric on the roll to see
whether it is washable or dry-cleanable only,
whether it is shrink resistant or stain resistant,
otherwise ask the salesperson. If the fabric is not
stain resistant, there are several firms that will
coat the fabric with a finish which does not allow
dust or dirt to penetrate. You can buy a fabric
protector in spray form, though this is a less
effective treatment. Use a gentle soap powder
when washing, and do not rub too vigorously in
case the texture is spoiled. Pressing should also
be undertaken with caution.

* washable with care. It is advisable to wash furnishing fabric before cutting to allow for shrinkage.
† dry clean only.

Baize†
A lightweight felted wool cloth, generally used to line cutlery drawers, the insides of cupboards, and to make cutlery bags.

Batik*
A fabric-dyeing technique where melted wax is painted on the fabric before dyeing and later removed to reveal the undyed areas, often resulting in a "smudgy" pattern. Usually in cotton, it is used for cushion covers, tablecloths, and wall hangings. Wash separately.

Blend (Union)†
The term given for the mixture of fibers – cotton/wool or linen/cotton. The effect is one of increased strength making it ideal for upholstery. Can sometimes be washed with care but dry cleaning is preferable.

Bouclé†
Fabric with a curled or looped surface, usually of heavier weight, suitable for upholstery.

Brocade†
A rich jacquard-woven fabric – it is a heavy fabric with an all-over raised design of silk texture on a matte background of different colors. Sumptuous looking, brocade is generally made of silk, rayon, and nylon yarns, often with a metallic treatment of gold or silver. Can be used for curtains or special upholstery.

Broderie Anglaise, Eyelet*
A cotton fabric in white or pastel colors with a lacy embroidered pattern, often cut out. Sometimes sold as a ruffle (frill) or trimming for a pillowcase or cushion.

Burlap (Hessian)†
A strong, coarse, loosely woven fabric, usually made from jute or hemp yarns. It is hard wearing but not successful as curtains. Better when dyed, paper-backed, and made into wallpaper. In upholstery, burlap (hessian) is used to cover the frame over the woven webbing as a platform for the stuffing.

Cambric†
A fine cotton that is plain woven and durable. It is often given a glaze and used for the inner cover of pillows, duvet covers, and cushions.

Candlewick*
A plain fabric with cotton tufts that form a pattern on the surface. It can be dyed into many colors and is used mainly for bedspreads.

Canvas†
A firm, heavy, strong, woven fabric, usually made from cotton. There is a host of weights and uses. It is sold bleached and unbleached.

Cheesecloth (Muslin)*
A soft, fine, very light fabric of cotton, or cotton mix. Can be stiffened. Swiss muslin is embroidered and used for the finishing touches in bedrooms – for lampshades, scatter cushions, or fine work. Not very durable but, depending on the finish, it can be carefully washed. Makes an economical draped window dressing or bed draping.

Chenille†
A cloth of heavily textured cotton or synthetic having rather a fuzzy decorative pile. Seen in highly ornamental trimmings.

Chintz†
A cotton fabric, traditionally printed with colorful patterns of flowers, fruits, and birds. Now commonly refers to glazed cotton in plain and patterns. Washing will remove the glaze. The only durable glazed chintz is one that is resin finished. Used for all soft furnishing purposes, including upholstery if backed with a lining. Some shrinkage if washed.

Corduroy†
This hard-wearing cloth is usually made of cotton, but also of synthetic yarns, all with a cotton-backing cloth. The cotton has cut-pile ribs, or cords, running down the length of the fabric which vary in width but are evenly spaced. Makes up well into curtains and upholstery giving a warm, comfortable feel. Interesting piping fabric if texture is wanted.

Cretonne†
A printed cotton without a glaze, available also in a twill. Heavier and more hardwearing than chintz, making it suitable for upholstery.

Crewelwork†
Crewel is a thin worsted yarn generally embroidered in chain stitch, stemstitch, or herringbone stitch onto white cotton or wool. Crewelwork often depicts a design such as the tree of life with bold curling leaves and exotic flowers. First used as early English and American hand-worked bed hangings, it is now available by the yard (meter) and can be used to make cushions and light upholstery, as well as curtains, wall hangings and bed drapes.

Damask†*
A firm self-patterned fabric made on a jacquard loom from cotton, linen, silk, rayon, or a combination of fibers. Traditionally used for table linen. The pattern is similar to brocade but flatter and reversible. The flat figuring is created by the contrast between the satin pattern and the matte finish of the background. This elegant fabric is used in restoration work, upholstering period pieces. Depending on the fiber used, it can be hard-wearing or delicate and should be used accordingly.

Decorator (Furnishing) Cotton*
A natural yarn woven into many qualities, some durable enough for upholstery, others as lightweight as voiles. Cotton dyes well and can be treated to produce finishes, such as creaseproof. When glazed it is easier to keep clean and holds its shape better. Blended with synthetic fibers for greater durability.

Domette†
Soft padded interlining fabric that is not as thick as wadding (bump). Used when the effect needed is one of a lightly padded curtain with a fine fabric. Also used when wadding (bump) would be too heavy.

Dupion, Douppioni†
Now produced from various fibers, although it was originally a fabric made from an irregular thickness of silks. Of medium weight with a slubbed appearance, dupion comes in many colors. Generally used for curtains.

Gaufrage†
The French word for embossing or stamping a pattern on cloth by means of heated rollers. Mostly done on velvet for upholstery. Avoid steam as the flattened design may disappear.

Georgette†*
A fine fabric with a crêpe texture, georgette is available in many fibers and drapes well. Comes in a wide range of colors; it is best used for sheer curtains, bed drapes, and Austrian shades (blinds).

Gingham*
A cotton fabric usually in a check pattern of two colors on white. Light and washable, it is often used in the kitchen, for table linen, and the furnishing of children's rooms.

Herringbone†
A twill weave achieved by alternating the diagonal pattern within the cloth. Suitable for upholstery, especially in wool or tweed.

Jacquard
A type of loom with a series of punched cards to control the weaving of the threads. The pattern usually has a multi-colored design and can be quite elaborate.

Lace*
A fine openwork fabric that usually comes in white with an applied pattern. Made of cotton or synthetic fibers. Can be used in windows instead of net curtains for privacy. Pretty as bed drapes and combined with Austrian shades (blinds). Other uses include romantic-style cushions, bedcovers, and dressing table skirts. Available in edgings and already gathered ruffles (frills).

Lawn*
A fine, light fabric, usually made of cotton but can be a linen or polyester yarn. It is semi-sheer and generally used for bed or table linen.

Linen†
A strong cloth that is spun from flax. It has a tendency to shrink and crease, limiting its use, but can be bought as a linen blend (union). This is a blend of cotton and linen, sometimes strengthened by a synthetic yarn. Frequently used as chair and sofa slipcovers, it does not soil quickly, comes in many colors, and is extremely hard wearing. Not recommended for curtains because it is rather stiff.

Lining*
A hard-wearing cotton fabric – sateen is the most popular – comes in all colors. Used to line curtains to protect the main fabric, add body, and help insulation. When making up curtains that are to be washed, be careful to use washable cotton lining, otherwise dry clean. Blackout lining, which has a metallic backing, is used where all light is to be cut out.

Linterfelt (Bump)†
Fibrous waste cotton wadding, commonly known as interlining (see page 29). Used between the back of the fabric and the lining to give bulk. It gives a rich full look, although it adds to the cost. In curtains linterfelt (bump) serves to block out some of the light and add to the insulation of the room. Be careful to consider carefully whether or not to put it in front of a radiator. It comes bleached and unbleached and has the appearance of a fluffy blanket.

Moiré†
A cotton, silk, or synthetic fabric which has a "watered" appearance. This comes in many weights of cloth, and there is an enormous range of colors for numerous uses. If washed, the watermark effect will disappear. Often seen on walls, in curtains, cushions, and light upholstery.

Muslin (Calico)*
Plain cotton fabric, strong but rather coarse. It is used for the platforms of dust ruffles (valances) and inner covers as an economy measure. Available in different weights, it shrinks when washed and never looks quite the same unless used on upholstery when it is tightly fitted. Takes stencils well, use fabric paints.

Net*
A fine, lightweight fabric, usually of synthetic yarn for soft furnishings. Available in pastel colors although, for a particularly dramatic effect, dark colors are available.

Organdy†
A very hard-wearing cotton cloth, which is very light, thin, transparent, and stiff. To be used when the effect to be created is of a slightly starched appearance.

Ottoman†
An increasingly sought-after cloth coming in many yarns – cotton, silk, and synthetic. It has a horizontal ribbed pattern and is suitable for upholstery as it is very hard wearing. Often to be found in stripes of different colors.

Percale*
A fine cotton, plain weave, used in the best-quality bedding. Also comes in a glazed finish.

Repp†
A strong, mono-colored ribbed cloth generally of cotton, lightly woven with the ribs running from selvage to selvage.

Sateen†
A lining fabric with a smooth, glazed, "satinized" finish, coming in a variety

of colors to match curtain fabric.

Satin†

A fabric made out of silk, cotton, or synthetic fibers. It is very smooth, soft, and shiny with a matte reverse side, often in lush, sometimes deep colors. Care should be taken when using this fabric, as it tends to spot and be difficult to clean.

Seersucker*

Easily identified by its puckered-and-flat appearance, often in checks or stripes. Generally cotton but available in other fibers. Washable but do not iron otherwise the effect is lost. If glazed, dry cleaning is advisable or the fabric will lose its body.

Shantung†

A plain woven fabric, often silk but sometimes a synthetic imitation. A slubbed appearance – short irregular thickened areas appearing in the cloth at irregular intervals. Used for cushions and elegant curtaining.

Sheeting*

Cotton or cotton blend fabric, sold in wider than normal widths so that it can be made up into bedclothes. Comes in a wide variety of patterns and colors.

Silk†

Regarded as the most luxurious of all fabrics. Coming in many forms, from fine linings to upholstery weight, in prints and colors, silk is soft, strong, and has an easily recognized character. It seldom clashes in color with another silk, meaning that it can be coordinated and, while appearing flimsy, if lined and interlined, it will last. Keep away from very strong direct light, as it fades. On these occasions it is wise to put up a window shade (blind) too. Dry clean in order to retain body. It has a variety of uses ranging from curtains, festoon shades (blinds), and tablecloths, to cushions, light upholstery, and lampshades.

Taffeta†

A fine plain weave fabric that is not particularly pliable. It used to be made only of silk but now comes in synthetics too. Many colors and smooth on both sides, usually with a sheen and sometimes "shot" in appearance, giving the effect that the fabric slightly changes color and appearance according to how the light falls on it. The "crunchy" feel of the fabric lends itself to Austrian shades (blinds).

Tapestry†

This is done traditionally either by hand or as jacquard-woven imitation. Coming in many colors and designs, it is commonly used for the upholstery of dining seats and other chairs, wall hangings, and mounting as cushions.

Terga (Ninon)†

A very light fabric, closely resembling a highly textured voile, it is found in synthetic form but is wonderful in silk. If used in great quantity, it has a light translucent appearance. This fabric should only be dry cleaned with great care otherwise it will lose its body. Can be used most effectively for festoon blinds anywhere where the desired effect is airy and light.

Ticking*

A heavy cotton twill, usually herringbone, either striped or a plain color. Used as the covering for mattresses or pillows as it is closely woven and the down or feather fillings cannot penetrate. Other uses are as an informal and hard-wearing upholstery cloth (deckchairs), or to put on the wall as a decorative covering.

Toile de Jouy†*

The name is given to printed cotton fabrics depicting pastoral scenes, usually of one color – shades of blue, red, or green. It originated in Jouy in France and was very popular in the eighteenth century. Often used as the upholstery on French-style chairs and charming as a decorative wall covering or curtaining.

Tweed†

A cloth made with wool yarns in a variety of weaves, textures, and colors. If used for curtains, the effect is one of informality and comfort, and when combined with tweed upholstery, the effect is one of warmth and comfort. The soft colors and weaves are good for accessories such a rugs, throws, and scatter cushions.

Twill†

The term given to the type of weave which produces diagonal lines within the fabric – herringbone being alternate diagonals. The cloth is hard wearing and is generally used for upholstery.

Velour†

A fabric with a thick pile that lies in one direction, made of cotton, wool, or synthetic fibers. Best suited for heavy, warm-looking, lush draperies and curtains or tablecloths.

Velvet†

A cut-pile cloth, woven with a thick short pile on one side only, made of cotton, wool, and synthetic fibers, coming in several weights and many colors. It is used for draping and upholstery although care should be taken to make sure that the pile is always lying in the same direction, otherwise the color looks different. It comes in medium and heavy weights.

Velveteen†

A weft-pile fabric that is brushed to resemble velvet.

Vinyl (PVC)

Now available in colors and patterns, ideal for tablecloths and padded (squab) seats in the kitchen, garden, and conservatory. As it is non-porous, it can be wiped clean.

Voile*

A cotton, silk, wool, or synthetic open-textured lightweight fabric that appears crisp and clear. Used as sheer curtains, festoons, and for draping furniture such as dressing tables and dust skirts (valances).

Worsted†

A hard-wearing wool fabric with a smooth texture. Useful for upholstery.

INDEX

ACKNOWLEDGMENTS

The producers and publishers would like to thank the following for their help in supplying their products for use in the photography:

Bernina (sewing machine); Byron & Byron (poles and finials); Cope & Timmins Ltd (curtain accessories); Wendy A Cushing Ltd (traditional cords and tassels); MacCulloch & Wallis (sewing equipment); Rufflette Ltd (curtain tapes and headings); Sleepeezee Ltd (bed); Warner Fabrics plc (fabrics)

Pictures

All photographs specially taken by Mark Gatehouse except for the following:

Guy Bouchet: page 177

Jane Churchill – The Summer Garden Collection: page 141 (above)

Jeremy Cockayne: page 134

Harry Cory-Wright: page 130

IPC Magazines/Robert Harding Syndication – 1988: page 174; 1989: pages 133, 142, 164; 1990: page 53; 1991: pages 52, 131 (left), 166

Maison de Marie Claire – photo: Hussenot/ stylist: Bayle/ Puech: pages 11, 145 (below); photo: Hussenot/ stylist: Puech: page 143 (below); photo: Dugied/ stylist: Postic: page 55

Fritz von der Schulenburg/Mimmi O'Connell: page 182

Stiebel of Nottingham: page 57 (above)

Elizabeth Whiting Agency: pages 1, 2, 10, 20 (above), 24, 34 (below), 42, 45 (top), 47, 51, 57 (below), 60, 68, 78, 87 (below), 90, 94, 99, 100, 101, 105, 132, 135, 136, 137, 140, 141 (below), 143 (above), 144, 146, 147, 162, 163, 165, 167, 168, 169, 172, 173, 175, 176, 178, 179

The World of Interiors/James Mortimer: pages 131 (right), 145 (above)